IF YOU
LIKE
METALLICA...

IF YOU LIKE METALLICA...

HERE ARE **OVER 200** BANDS, CDS, MOVIES, AND OTHER ODDITIES THAT YOU WILL LOVE

MIKE McPADDEN

Backbeat
Books

AN IMPRINT OF HAL LEONARD CORPORATION

Published in 2012 by Backbeat Books
An Imprint of Hal Leonard Corporation
7777 West Bluemound Road
Milwaukee, WI 53213

Trade Book Division Editorial Offices
33 Plymouth St., Montclair, NJ 07042

Book design by Michael Kellner

Printed in the United States of America

Library of Congress Cataloging-in-Publication Data

McPadden, Mike.
If you like Metallica : here are over 200 bands, CDs, movies, and other oddities that you will love / Mike McPadden.
    p. cm.
Includes bibliographical references and index.
1. Metallica (Musical group) 2. Heavy metal music--Miscellanea. I. Title.
ML421.M48M36 2012
782.42166092'2--dc23
                        2012003529

ISBN 978-1-61713-038-0

www.backbeatbooks.com

CONTENTS

Metallica, circa 1986: Cliff Burton, Kirk Hammett, Lars Ulrich, and James Hetfield. (Elektra/Photofest)

Introduction

IF YOU LIKE METALLICA...
YOU'VE COME TO THE RIGHT BOOK

I like Metallica.

I like them now, at press time, post-Lou Reed and working on their tenth studio album.

I liked them when I first heard *Kill 'Em All* in early 1983, during my initial attempt, at fourteen, to go headbanger. My big move from FM radio rock to underground metal and extreme noise, though, got postponed for a spell by a headily all-consuming fixation on Rush and Pink Floyd (ignited in no small part by weekend-long bong-hit-and-Whip-It festivals at my friend Vito's house).

I also liked Metallica in 1991, when they tossed their leather charms into the ring against grunge (which, sort of like Metallica itself, began as a mix of Sabbath and the Stooges) and the more suspect "alternative rock" (which, unlike Metallica, descended from the punk-empowered New Wave of British Heavy Metal, descended from plain-old punk-castrating New Wave).

I very much liked how, at the end of the decade, a group whose name begins with "m-e-t-a-l" emerged as the most popular hard rock act of all time.

In 1986, however, I really fell in love with Metallica. I was eighteen and had attempted to fully embrace punk rock, but I could not stand the orthodoxy. I loved Fear and the Sex Pistols and I didn't understand why, then, that meant I had to deny the sheer might of AC/DC and Judas Priest. At the same time, metal severely tested my ability to relate to wizardry and dragon-slaying.

Remember, now, that "the crossover" had not yet occurred—at least not where I was from, in Flatbush, Brooklyn. Locally, Black Flag bars could get you a motorcycle boot to the medulla oblongata at metal mecca L'Amour, while wearing Black Sabbath patch at a CBGB hardcore matinee was just asking for dental work via Doc Martens.

Two exceptions existed: the Ramones, sort of, and Motörhead, for sure. So I was putzing around Washington Square park one class-cutting afternoon in a motorcycle jacket emblazoned with Ramones buttons and a huge Motörhead boar-of-war-face I'd painted on the back (under which I added the Monkees logo, just to be the way I was, and am).

Then, into my line of site sashayed a Mohawk-coifed, nasally safety-pinned, plaid-skirted, bondage-booted beauty about my age who had completed her seamlessly punk ensemble with . . . a Metallica shirt?!?!

Specifically, it was a *Ride the Lightning* tee, and, even more specifically, she wore no bra in order to make bobblingly clear that she'd been pierced in places that were really wild to get pierced circa 1986.

Did I approach this vision? Of course not. I was me. At eighteen. Instead, I beelined it to Tower Records and snagged, on cassette, the recently released *Master of Puppets*.

There, at last, I heard the music I didn't even know I had only previously been hoping would one day exist. It was metal. It was punk. It was about being the type of dope who, upon seeing his idea of an ideal girl in an ideal circumstance, deals with it by running off to a record store. It was perfect.

I arrived (relatively) late to Revolution Metallica, but I stayed permanently.

Okay, pretty much permanently.

As with all passions, especially with rock groups whose tenure spans decades, periods arose along the way where liking Metallica proved, let's say, queasy-making—not just for me, but for the band members themselves (just ask James Hetfield about Lars Ulrich and Kirk Hammett's late-'90s experiments with guyliner).

I come to praise Metallica in this book, though, not to mention Napster and/or the Andres Serrano cover load on *Load* and/or the absence of guitar solos on *St. Anger* and/or their group therapist's Cosby sweaters in *Some Kind of Monster*.

Let us focus instead on how, with *Death Magnetic*, in 2008 Metallica reconnected with and became reinvigorated by everything there ever was to like about them and, by extension, all of hard rock and heavy metal.

Death Magnetic also reminded us that before Metallica was the biggest metal band in the world, they were the biggest metal *fans* in the world.

Metallica came to be as a result of teenage obsessives bonding over their love of heavy music to the point that they could no longer just listen. They had to join in and contribute to the racket and the ruckus. It just so happened that these particular zit-faced wastrels would pack the biggest, and best, punch at the entire blowout.

From power chord one onward, Metallica explicitly saluted the existing talents that inspired them and sought out new compatriots and contemporaries in order to build a more perfect means of moving the music forward.

This book examines those artists—mostly rock performers, but also filmmakers, painters, and a writer or two—who contributed profoundly to making Metallica, in all its forms, into Metallica.

If you like Metallica, you will read here about a lot of things that the members of Metallica like. You will also read about musicians and other phenomena that are in keeping with the Metallica way of life, be it through direct connections, philosophical similarities, or a simple ability to kick your ass the way *Master of Puppets* kicked mine in 1986.

There's a lot to like here (I hope). Go, now, and kill 'em all.

Black Sabbath, 1970. (Photofest)

1

BATTERY: CHANNELING THE POWER OF OLD GODS

In the beginning, giants smashed the earth. There was heavy before metal, and then metal made everything heavier. The giants took tee elements on as both their outward armor and the molten lifeblood racing through their systems—all of it, heavy metal.

The form arose, full blown, with Black Sabbath, but Birmingham, UK's bleakest burbled to the tar pit surface on the backs of acid-ossified bell-bottom brigands and electric-blues buccaneers before them. From Sabbath, then, came all ensuing heaviosity and metallicism.

Members of the first generation are Metallica's original forebears: the titans, the heroes, the founders, the originals. The old gods.

Gather for services.

AC/DC

In *Rock and the Pop Narcotic,* author Joe Carducci nails Australian rabble-rousers AC/DC with a single caption. Under a shot of the band in action, Carducci writes: "Perfect. Not a brain cell to spare."

The notion that heavy metal is "dumb" music for "dumb" people is a charge that has stuck since the first time Black Sabbath frightened the chamomile tea out of *Rolling Stone*'s review staff. At the time, the writers' only defense mechanism was exactly that of the playground bully victim: to dismiss the new threat as "stupid" and "jerky" and even, albeit via a whole lot more words, "poopy-headed."

Carducci's description of the hive mind behind "She's Got Balls," "Big Balls," and *Ballbreaker* as operating at its full intellectual capacity is no slight, though: He is, in fact, saluting AC/DC as a raw beast of unadulterated, all-cylinders rock 'n' roll.

For AC/DC, there are no distractions, no pretensions, no misunderstandings. The music directly conveys the purity of hard rock at its hardest and most rocking. Every crunching electric-blues riff, over-the-falls-without-a-barrel solo, and chant-along vocal encapsulates the sex of violence and the violence of sex. It's dirty music for bad boys to dance to with dangerous women. Especially in the sack.

The leer in many a James Hetfield delivery and the singular focus of Metallica at its most effective comes from plugging into the endless power source that is AC/DC.

Heavy metal as scary music for scary people is a charge that holds more weight. And AC/DC, although so beloved now that they once even got to have their own shopping department in Wal-Mart, definitely started out scary.

A lot of the fear factor had to do with that aforementioned carnality. But, careening off what Black Sabbath had wrought, AC/DC flirted sufficiently with demonic imagery from its 1975 debut *High Voltage* onward to spawn the endearing myth that their name is an abbreviation of "After Christ/Devil Comes" or "Anti-Christ/Devil Child."

The occult ruminations culminated with the 1979 album *Highway to Hell*, on the cover of which manic midget guitar-genius Angus Young brandishes red horns. Smiling to his left is lead singer Bon Scott, who, on the hit title track, wails to his own mother and Satan himself about the inevitability of the rock 'n' roll outlaw's infernal eternal hereafter.

On February 19, 1980, Bon Scott hit that road for real. His coroner's report cites "acute alcohol poisoning" and "death by misadventure."

AC/DC honored their fallen front man by soldiering onward, as all-systems-always-on-full-go Scott surely would have insisted they do. Gravel-gargling shriek-master Brian Johnson of glam-rockers Geordie took the mic, and just five months later, the band delivered

Back in Black. To date, only Michael Jackson's *Thriller* keeps it from being the best-selling album of all time.

The lessons of AC/DC surely hung heavy on Metallica in September 1986, following the death of Cliff Burton. Just as Bon Scott had been AC/DC's frontline personality, Burton served as Metallica's soul. To break up the band and end any further development of what a fallen member had worked so hard to create hardly seemed a fitting tribute. Metallica therefore welcomed Jason Newsted to the fold and went on to become the biggest hard rock band that ever existed.

Hell's bells ring eternal.

AEROSMITH

Some bands you listen to. Others feel like they've been listening to you.

For young James Hetfield, Aerosmith topped the list of artists who fit into the latter category. They were the single outfit above all others that inspired him to take up guitar playing. Musically, then, Aerosmith is a crucial factor in Metallica. But they influenced the band in other ways, too.

As a teenager, Hetfield wrote personal letters to Aerosmith leaders Steven Tyler and Joe Perry. Instead of even a casual response, Hetfield only ever got back an order form for Aerosmith merchandise. He recalls it as an example of how *not* to treat fans.

On their way to the top, where they surpassed even Aerosmith, Metallica enjoyed a face-to-face rapport with fans that fueled much of their success, extending from open-ended meet and greets to encouragement of tape trading. That changed, of course, with Metallica's Napster freak-out in 2000, but it was phenomenal while it lasted. Profitable, too.

The parallels between Aerosmith and Metallica, who played together numerous times over the past thirty years, are manifold. Each was the biggest American hard rock juggernaut of its heyday. Each bent styles to re-create and redefine its existing genre. Each has distinct phases of success. And each is fronted by a two-headed human typhoon comprised of mighty men who come off as gods, geniuses, visionaries, and jerks—sometimes (many times) all at once.

Aerosmith burst out of Boston in 1970, a fat-bottomed boogie-woogie amalgam of the Stones, Hendrix, glam rock, and their own fire-fingered, rubber-lipped originality.

The aforementioned Tyler and Perry, on vocals and guitar respectively, immediately rivaled Mick Jagger and Keith Richards as hard-living, harder-rocking brothers-in-arms whose (chemical-clogged) limbs would often flail asunder into decidedly unbrotherly fisticuffs. Not for nothing were they deemed "the Toxic Twins."

That two-headed, louder-than-lust, heavier-than-hate dynamic is mirrored, of course, in Metallica's Hetfield and Lars Ulrich.

In the manner that heavy metal band Metallica openly embraced punk, Aerosmith reignited itself, phoenixlike, by gambling on rap. In retrospect, Tyler's motormouthed delivery on the 1977 smash "Walk This Way" sounds like proto-hip-hop mic fronting. Clearly, Run-DMC—whose trailblazing first records contained myriad metal riffs—picked up on this. The two groups' collaborative cover of "Walk This Way" in 1986 stormed the pop charts, remade nigh-extinct dinosaurs Aerosmith as MTV superstars, and, in fact, did nothing short of utterly upend popular culture.

After their comeback, Aerosmith were determined in no uncertain terms to stay on top. Over the next twenty years they delivered impeccably crafted nuggets of video-friendly hard-pop gold and power ballads teens could dance to with their grandmas. Yet to everybody but those in the metal underworld who had stopped buying their records anyway, all this proud sellout maneuvering somehow only made Aerosmith seem cooler.

Metallica followed Aerosmith's lead throughout the '90s. The Black Album propelled them to unprecedented heights at the beginning of the decade, and they made sure they only went up from there—cutting their hair, softening their sound, and starring in slick, sometimes even cute, videos. Lars Ulrich wore makeup and got photographed tongue-kissing Kirk Hammett. James went to a dermatologist.

When accused of being sellouts, Metallica's go-to retort became: "Damn right! We sell out every night!"

Come the turn of the twenty-first century, both Aerosmith and Metallica would undergo core-shattering changes. Drugs, fights, bomb records, fan alienation, and personal breakdowns made for several nasty, nearly lethal seasons amidst each camp.

In time, Metallica reconvened and released *Death Magnetic* in 2008, at once a return home and a hard leap forward.

Aerosmith remains a question mark, but Steven Tyler has proven to be an instant TV legend as a judge on *American Idol*.

The same could certainly not be said for Jason Newsted in his 2006 stint on CBS's *Rockstar: Supernova*.

So the two bands still do have some serious differences, after all.

BLACK SABBATH

Friday the 13th. February 1970. *Black Sabbath*, the album, is released by Black Sabbath, the band, commencing with a song titled "Black Sabbath."

All hell breaks loose.

"Emerging like the monolith in Stanley Kubrick's *2001: A Space Odyssey*," Ian Christe writes in *Sound of the Beast*, "Black Sabbath was as irreducible as the bottomless sea, the everlasting sky, the mortal soul . . . a death knell for the music known as rock and roll, which would forever after be merely the domesticated relative of heavy metal."

Practitioners and enthusiasts of electric blues, acid rock, prog, psychedelia, and all fringe variations of amplified music heeded the call: "Gentlemen, turn upside-down your crosses!" (Ladies got the invite, too, beckoned by the green-skinned enchantress on Black Sabbath's instantly iconic cover.)

So: no Black Sabbath, no heavy metal, no Metallica, no book in your hands right now (or at least not this one; might I suggest something else from the esteemed Backbeat library?).

Metallica is the biggest heavy metal band of all time. But Black Sabbath was the first biggest heavy metal band of all time—and they're still, as Metallica vociferously points out whenever possible, the heaviest and most metal.

Inducting Black Sabbath into the Rock and Roll Hall of Fame in 2006, Lars Ulrich addressed the group's four original members: "Bill, Geezer, Ozzy, and Tony, if it weren't for you, we wouldn't be here. I hereby not only acknowledge but scream from every fucking rooftop, 'Black Sabbath *is* and always will be synonymous with the term 'heavy metal'!'"

Added James Hetfield (tearfully, in spots): "Picture a nine-year-old boy, quiet, well-behaved on the outside, but on the inside boiling and dying for life to burst open. The discovery of music was what burst it open. But not any music, this was more than just music—a powerful, loud, heavy sound that moved his soul. This timid nine-year-old constantly raided his older brother's record collection. He was drawn to them like a magnet to metal . . . more like a shy boy to his own loud voice. Those monstrous riffs lived inside him and spoke the feelings he could never put into words. They helped crack the shell he was stuck in. Also, scaring his mom and sister was an extra bonus."

Hetfield, of course, was the kid, but that very experience is shared, to a black T-shirt and horned hand salute, among his entire generation of metal fans and musicians alike—much the way *Kill 'Em All* blew minds among tenderfoot headbangers in 1981 and the Black Album did for the rest of the rock audience a decade later.

In concert, Metallica routinely bursts into impromptu bits of Sabbath songs between numbers—a bit of "Iron Man" here, thirty seconds of "Symptom of the Universe" there. For their 1998 covers album *Garage Inc.*, Metallica chose "Sabbra Cadabra" and, without explicitly pointing it out, a sizable hunk of "A National Acrobat."

Both originals come from 1973's semi-experimental wing stretcher *Sabbath Bloody Sabbath*. It was the first album on which the unholy quartet incorporated strings and orchestral touches— a move that would presage Metallica's oeuvre in the '90s—and thereby melted (some) hearts of rock reviewers who had previously only exhibited icy hatred. Even *Rolling Stone* raved about *Sabbath Bloody Sabbath*. That positive note would be the first and, for a long time, the last when it came to the magazine's opinion on the band.

"Sabbra Cadabra" crystallizes the new direction. It commences with a boogie riff and happy lyrics about lovin' a lady that makes you feel "all riiiiiight!" Then it heads into a tunnel of Moog synthesizer madness, a blues breakdown, honky-tonk piano flourishes, and semi-samba percussion. Ozzy, wailing higher than when he was feeling high in the first part, sounds sad as he promises repeatedly he won't leave this lady "no more, no more, uh no more, I said nooooo more!"

"A National Acrobat" sounds more like traditional Sabbath but, from its title to its echoing-into-eternity vibe, it's even weirder.

Metallica does away with the extra instruments, but it's intriguing as to why, from the entire Sabbath catalogue, they'd pick "Sabbra Cadabra" and "A National Acrobat." *Garage Inc.* aimed to do for U2-caliber Metallica what *Garage Days Re-Revisited* had done for the post–*Master of Puppets* ragamuffins: show the band returning to basics, relearning (and re-teaching) ancient lessons, and cleaning the slate to start anew.

Perhaps implied from the endlessly charming title, "Sabbra Cadabra" provides a robust example of the original masters showing off their full complement of tricks. "A National Acrobat"—which Metallica tears into, unannounced, in the middle of "Sabbra"—is all about reincarnation.

Metallica had led numerous lives by 1998—first as metalhead punks with Dave Mustaine and Cliff Burton, then as ascending underworld champions with Jason Newsted, and then it was all sunglasses, funny cars, art auctions, and Hollywood.

The uncredited insertion of "A National Acrobat" announces the death of Metallica at the top of the entire rock game, with a promise of rebirth to come. It would take six years, and the result would be the mutant miscarriage *St. Anger*, and then they would have to do it again (*Some Kind of Monster*) and again (*Death Magnetic*), but the endless cycle of Metallica's life is all in there—life spawned by Black Sabbath.

Talk about killing yourself to live.

BOB SEGER

It seemed a curious match—Metallica covering Bob Seger's "Turn the Page" on *Garage Inc.*—despite Lars Ulrich bringing the song to the band after hearing it while driving and thinking the song could easily have been written by James Hetfield.

In fact, Metallica's lead singer didn't have particularly generous words for its originator, and even claimed he didn't know who it was.

"I heard a song on the radio singing about the road life," Hetfield said, "a kind of somber, gruff, honest lyric in there. I kind of felt it could be Bob Seger, but the lyric and song itself were great. So it's all to do with that song rather than Bob Seger itself. The lyrics are us. We've been road dogs since day one."

Metallica's "Turn the Page," backed by a video featuring '80s porn star Ginger Lynn as a put-upon stripper mom, proved to be one of the band's most instantly popular hits.

It also added another platinum brick to the pantheon of songs by rich and famous rock stars about how bad it sucks to be a rich and famous rock star (see, in addition, "The Ballad of John and Yoko" by the Beatles, "Limelight" by Rush, "Lodi" by Creedence Clearwater Revival, and so on).

Given Seger's semi-uncool status as the lone corporately salable nugget of the late-'60s Detroit scene that also launched the Stooges and MC5, coupled with his exhausting omnipresence on FM radio, Hetfield's semi-embarrassed justification of the cover is kind of understandable.

Only it's not.

It's not, because Bob Seger really was a peer of Iggy and Fred "Sonic" Smith, and the 1969 album *Ramblin' Gamblin' Man* by the Bob Seger System is a slab of proto-metal garage rock on par with the most ferocious offerings of its time and place.

The familiar title track smokes enough, but the record's cult item "2+2=?" is an antiwar scorcher unequaled anywhere in popular music until the coming of "One" by Metallica.

Amidst a trudging bass, a hypnotic wah-wah guitar lick, and racing-round-your-skull stereo effects, "2+2"'s lyrics challenge the concept of drafting the young into combat, sung from the point of view of an angry protagonist who'd fit perfectly anywhere in the Metallica canon—but especially as one of the "disposable heroes" buried on the cover of *Master of Puppets*. After being dumped into the mud and blood of a war he doesn't understand in a world he'll never comprehend, the protagonist states: "Ask what answer I can find? I ain't saying I'm a genius. Two plus two is on my mind."

The song's title evokes a grapple with common sense: If you're being asked to kill and die for reasons that no one can explain, then perhaps none of life's fundamentals hold true. Maybe 2+2 doesn't equal what it's supposed to. Maybe it never did.

By 1996, Metallica may have identified with the Bob Seger of "Turn the Page," but the 1969 Bob Seger of "2+2=?" embodies the spirit that Metallica rode (the lightning) hard in order to get to that point.

Hear it and weep.

BLUE ÖYSTER CULT

Blue Öyster Cult is weird.

First, there's the name.

Then it's weird that they came from that hotbed of hard rock experimentation, Stony Brook University in suburban Long Island circa 1967. (It wasn't actually a hotbed of hard rock experimentation.)

It's further weird that this early juggernaut of rock criticism's least favorite genre—heavy metal—had rock critic Sandy Pearlman as their Svengali and rock critic Richard Meltzer as a frequent lyricist, and that still more lyrics came from rock critic darlings Patti Smith and Jim Carroll.

Then there are the members: E. Bloom on vocals, Buck Dharma on guitar, and, for a quick stint circa 1983, *American Idol* judge Randy Jackson on bass. Weirdos. The lot of them.

The band's subject matter is science fiction, Zen consciousness, interdimensional mysticism and, at least once, the nobility of the Canadian Mountie. Their sound—lilting and spacey at some points, scary and barbaric at others—is sort of like the Byrds, sort of like Alice Cooper, and sort of like the Mahavishnu Orchestra, each of whom they toured with early.

It's a weird pedigree.

Weirdest of all is that all this weirdness worked. By 1976, BÖC were packing arenas and racking up gold records, and scored had a deathless radio hit (about Death Itself) with "Don't Fear the Reaper" (also known, to at least one entire generation, as "More Cowbell").

For a while, they made good on manager Pearlman's hope that the band would be America's answer to Black Sabbath (even touring with the Dio-fronted lineup in 1980). BÖC, in fact, remained one of rock's top acts for a solid decade after their breakthrough.

What's not weird is that Blue Öyster Cult made such an indelible impact on the up-and-strumming members of Metallica.

BÖC's succession of radio-ready crop dusters instantly seduced teenage burnouts through sheer force of riffage. The apocalyptic implications of such titles as "Cities on Flame with Rock-n-Roll," "Godzilla," "Burnin' for You," and "Dancin' in the Ruins" are actually topped by how hard and heavy the songs come tumbling down upon the listener, each and every go-round.

These instant transport devices served as gateways into BÖC's more heady and ethereal material: galaxy-spanning journeys and meditations more than hazardous than Hawkwind, more perilous than Pink Floyd.

On *Garage Inc.*, Metallica chose to cover one such time- and space-bending nugget: "Astronomy," from the 1974 Blue Öyster Cult album *Secret Treaties*. It's about a mutant human guided to various star outposts by invisible aliens as they explain his role in the universe.

Again: weird. Again: awesome. Again: only Blue Öyster Cult. But this time by way of Metallica.

As noted, the megalithic success of Blue Öyster Cult did not run on into infinity. By 2000, when the band clocked in at #55 on VH1's *100 Greatest Artists of Hard Rock*, they were playing small theaters and county fairs.

Let's let this poignant quote from James Hetfield end the BÖC segment: "They were headlining stadiums and now they do clubs, and [I think], 'How can they do that?' I go and see them, and I see, in their eyes, that they love playing, and it don't matter where they're playing! And that's what it's all about."

They are the cosmos.

COVEN

Nineteen sixty-nine was the moment when the Age of Aquarius corroded into the Season of the Witch. Following the Summer of Love and Woodstock's three days of peace and music, '69 went out with the Manson murders, the Rolling Stones' lethal Altamont concert, and a major-label record release containing occult rituals, satanic invocations, a musician named Oz Osbourne, and an opening number titled "Black Sabbath."

No, this album was not *Black Sabbath* by Black Sabbath. That came in 1970. The groundbreaker at cloven hoof here is *Witchcraft Destroys Minds and Reaps Souls* by Coven, a group of Chicago rock-sorcerers whose bassist just happened to go by the name Oz Osbourne. That the record starts with "Black Sabbath" as well is simply freaky.

Thematically, Coven focused on dark arts, hellfire, and unholy outrage. Aesthetically, the entire focus zeroed in on lead singer Jinx Dawson, an ice-blonde Nordic beauty trained in opera and otherworldly communion who mesmerized audiences to the point of possession.

Jinx, who anointed herself the "Goth Queen" back when the term had more to do with Visigoths than Manic Panic hair dye, even appears full-frontal nude on the album's inner gatefold, serving as a sacrificial altar for the band in full black magic resplendence.

On the road, Coven toured with proto-metal giants Alice Cooper, the Yardbirds, and Vanilla Fudge. So, in heavy metal history annals, why do we not hear more about this anti-goddess and her hooded cabal?

The issue is, well, the music.

Witchcraft Destroys Minds and Reaps Souls might boast song titles on the order of "Dignitaries of Hell," "Pact with Lucifer" (hilariously misspelled on the jacket as "Pack with Lucifer"), and (brace yourself, Van Hagar fans) "For Unlawful Carnal Knowledge," but it sounds like . . . hippie stuff.

Side one is kind of folk, kind of prog, and a whole lot of late-'60s pop. Side two contains no music at all, save for occasional chanting, as it purports to be the first-ever commercially available recording of an actual black mass.

Still, the (proudly) damned thing is all about evil, and it's sung by the Goth Queen, and it features "Oz Osbourne" jamming on "Black Sabbath"! As such, Coven is a key preceding ripple in the primordial glop from which Black Sabbath, the band, would emerge a year hence, carrying with it all heavy metal that would ever proceed forward, including, of course, Metallica.

After their self-titled 1971 follow-up LP, Coven fizzled out. For all the insistent naked-lady devil-worship histrionics, however, Coven pulled off a real shocker by achieving immortality as one of AM radio pop's great one-hit wonders.

The song is "One Tin Soldier." It's the theme to the iconic counterculture drive-in-flick-turned blockbuster *Billy Jack* (1971), and it's one hell of a ditty (pun, as always, intended).

Billboard-chart friendly or not, "One Tin Soldier" is perfectly in keeping with both Coven's hatred of religious hypocrisy and Billy Jack's socking it to the establishment in a matter that ultimately would mesh perfectly with Metallica's worldview.

In fact, Billy Jack could be a character in Metallica song. He's a Green Beret Vietnam vet who fights for peace-loving Indians and teenage castoffs by kicking the crap out of racist, rapist rednecks.

The movie describes him as "a war hero who hated the war," making Billy Jack a forebear of the now two generations (and counting) of American troops who have rolled into Middle East combat to the tune of Metallica's numerous antiwar anthems.

Metallica has always made it clear that they love these fighters, no matter how much quarrel they have with any particular fight.

As for the message of the song, "One Tin Soldier" spins a yarn about valley folk and mountain people, the latter of whom have offered to share their "treasure" with the former. The valley folk get greedy, though, and massacre their mountain brethren, only to discover that the treasure in question is the simple statement "Peace on earth."

James Hetfield one day would write epics just as acidic and

stingingly cynical. But no way would he look as good splayed out naked on a human-sacrifice table.

DEEP PURPLE

Go ahead, ask Deep Purple organist Jon Lord if he's ever played in a heavy metal band. "Never," Lord told *Kerrang!* magazine. "We never wore studded wristbands or posed for photos with blood pouring out of our mouths. That's okay. That's for people who are into a different kind of music to us."

That was in 1982, a decade after the blacker-than-a-bottomless pit, more-monstrous-than-the-mightiest-behemoth thirteen opening notes of Deep Purple's "Smoke on the Water" defined the heavy metal riff from first pick stroke unto eternity.

Sorry, Jon—if the dragon-tooth platform boot fits . . .

Heavy metal gods Led Zeppelin are not actually "heavy metal," per se, either, but not for nothing did both those bands, then and now, get automatically grouped alongside Black Sabbath.

Alas, in 1972, *The Guinness Book of World Records* certified Deep Purple, the brainchild of session player turned guitar sorcerer Ritchie Blackmore, as "the world's loudest pop group."

Hard charging straightaway, Deep Purple took several albums and lineups to perfect its metal-foundation-laying incarnation. Blackmore recruited bassist Roger Glover and vocalist Ian Gillan from Episode Six for 1970's *Deep Purple in Rock* LP and, well, all involved lived up to the album's title.

Two mega-albums followed, *Fireball* and *Machine Head*, the latter of which contains "Smoke on the Water," "Highway Star," and "Space Truckin'." Wrap your (machine) head around that.

Blackmore's leads and solos exist in the rarified air of the greats, while Lord's virtuoso keyboards are a wonder unto themselves. Singer Gillan continuously erupts into impossible ranges that metal front men forever after have sought to emulate (in 1971, Purple lent Gillan out to perform the title role on the original concept album version of *Jesus Christ Superstar*—his prowess does the part divine justice).

Typical turmoil tore Deep Purple asunder, with Blackmore splitting to form Rainbow and Gillan being replaced by David

Coverdale, with all the standard-issue VH1 *Behind the Music* tumult.

In one form or another, the band kept chugging.

The classic lineup reunited in 1984 and scored a hit ("Knockin' on Your Back Door"). Then it blew apart again. But, still, forty-plus-years in, Deep Purple (occasionally) performs and (less occasionally) records.

As their powers peaked in 1971, grade-schooler Lars Ulrich snagged a ticket to a Purple gig in Copenhagen. His tender mind, as you might imagine, was entirely blown.

Later, he'd stake out what hotel the band was staying out while in town and wait for hours in the lobby to meet the members.

Diamond Head's Brian Tatler recalls a teenage Lars endlessly watching and re-watching a Betamax tape of Deep Purple at the 1974 Cal Jam, aping every lick.

In 2006, after Metallica was inducted into the Rock and Roll Hall of Fame, a reporter asked who he'd like to see honored next. "I'd say Deep Purple," Lars said. "If you say Led Zeppelin and Black Sabbath, you also have to say Deep Purple. They come as a threesome."

Even today, Ulrich names Purple's 1972 live collection *Made in Japan* as his all-time favorite album.

Less familiar, but obviously a profound influence on not just Lars but all his bandmates, was Deep Purple's 1970 *Concerto for Group and Orchestra*. It's just what it sounds like: *Deep Purple* jamming with a full classical ensemble—a major precursor to *S&M: Symphony and Metallica* in 1999.

Throughout the many stages of its evolution, Metallica has burst into Deep Purple covers from their earliest club gigs to the biggest festivals, even recording "Black Night" for a fan club CD.

So cut them any way you like, Metallica proves time and again that the band's life essence bleeds Deep Purple.

DUST

Despite their sound (barbarian metal by way of Blue Cheer, ELP, and Flatbush, Brooklyn) and their imagery (barbarian metal by way of mummified skeletons of ancient Rome and the genius brushstrokes of fellow Brooklyn boy Frank Frazetta), there is something engagingly punk rock about Dust—and not just because their drummer grew up to be Marky Ramone.

They were three scrappy, scraggly youngsters out of New York City's same County of Kings that was simultaneously whelping forth Sir Lord Baltimore. Richie Wise handled vocals and guitar, Kenny Aaronson played bass, and fifteen-year-old Marc Bell (later Ramone) managed the drums (he was actually thirteen when the band started gigging).

Hard Attack, Dust's 1972 effort, is a masterpiece of brawn, passion, and invention. Sometimes it sounds like Cream or Mountain—with words that recall the best of what Bernie Taupin was supplying to Elton John at the time—but most often, Dust just sounds like something it should be impossible for a trio of teens to accomplish. *Hard Attack* went gold, and you can hear why.

The album's interludes into quiet reflection build to one of early metal's most bruising punch-outs, "Suicide." It's a four-and-a-half minute reign of fuzz-box terror punctuated throughout out by Bell's one-brass-knuckle-at-a-time drum cascades and, smack in the middle, the most legitimately psychotic bass solo prior to Cliff Burton's "(Anesthesia) Pulling Teeth."

The aforementioned punkiness of Dust comes not so much from their music but from the fact that they were out-of-sorts teenagers who assembled out of a sheer love of hard rock and tapped into a much larger moment that expanded into a movement. That's how the Ramones did it (with original drummer Tommy Ramone) five years later, and that's how Metallica did it five years after that.

JIMI HENDRIX

People played electric guitars prior to Jimi Hendrix, but every note to emerge from every electric guitar since Hendrix has been a direct descendent of this infinite-fingered afro-voodoo deity.

Similarly, there was hard rock before Hendrix—the Stones, the Who, Cream, Blue Cheer—but then in 1967 came the album *Are You Experienced?* and with it "Purple Haze," "Foxy Lady," and the title track. Hard rock solidified and took flight.

It wasn't just that Hendrix changed the language of the six strings, it was as though he blew apart the discussion with an entirely new alphabet. If you had a guitar, you immediately had to learn the vocabulary and see how you could add to the lexicon.

And if you didn't have a guitar . . . well, then, at least you could drop a lot of acid and tune in, turn on, and—using whatever you thought was in your hands—wail out.

The power of Hendrix is such, though, that hallucinogens are not necessary to simply "trip" on his music (they don't exactly hurt, either). Just ask Kirk Hammett.

Hammett is a Hendrix fanatic whose in-concert cover of Hendrix's "Little Wing" is a highlight of the Metallica video *Live Shit: Binge & Purge*. It's taken from a 1989 show in Seattle, Jimi's hometown. Love oozes from every lick.

KISS

"You wanted the best . . . you got the best! The hottest band in the world . . . *Kiss*!"

That onstage proclamation famously kicks off 1975's watershed two-record set *Kiss Alive!*

As the crowd explodes upon the opening of "Deuce," it's clear they really do want Kiss. The face paint. The flames. The leather. The boots. The tongue. The whole spook-house-UFO-Kabuki-superhero freak show.

Who could resist?

Certainly not anybody who grew up to play in Metallica.

Kiss is the bridge between Black Sabbath and bubblegum. It's great hard rock that goes down easy and feels good all over. It kicks your ass, but you can shake your groove thing to it, too.

Song by song, Kiss conveys the boot-stomp joy of Sweet and Slade by way of the nastiness of the Stones, the vastness Led Zeppelin, and the mutant flair (and more than a little makeup) of Alice Cooper. They boast four personalities as original and distinct as the Monkees, but they rock way harder—for the exact same audience.

Yet for all those intoxicating outside ingredients, Kiss is a brew like no other.

The band infiltrated the mainstream with dark and diabolical concepts and rhythms—naturally (perhaps even calculatedly) inviting rumors they were Knights In Satan's Service—but they did so with fire-breathing fun and supersonic good-time vibrations that served to sell dolls, comic books, lunchboxes, trading cards, pinball machines, and all other conceivable childhood ephemera to which a price tag could be affixed. (The eventual advent of Kiss coffins meant that the ultimate capitalist rock 'n' roll juggernaut could now, in a very real sense, carry fans from cradle to grave.)

Again, though, what transcends mere dollar value is the actual music.

When junior-high-era Hetfield, Ulrich, and company first laid hands on workable instruments, it was Kiss riffs that rang in their heads. Of course, our boys (especially Lars, one suspects) also learned a thing or two (billion) from Simmons & Stanley Inc. about the big business of being in the biggest band in the world.

Of special note in a Metallica context is that Kiss forged their own phenomenon, both musical and monetary, in the face of blatant hostility from respectable mainstream tastemakers and an absolute freeze-out from rock radio.

When the word *Metallica* finally made the cover of *Rolling Stone* in 1989, it was followed, accurately, by the tagline "The Top 10 Band You Won't Hear on the Radio."

Implicit there (although, *Rolling Stone* being *Rolling Stone*, unacknowledged) is that Metallica got where they were because Kiss first showed them—and everybody else—how it's done.

All night and ev-uh-ree day.

LED ZEPPELIN

The ultimate heavy metal band is not actually heavy metal.

Led Zeppelin swooped hard rock to unparalleled heights in its ascent and dominance of the 1970s, soaring—arms outstretched in a simultaneous gesture of conquest and embrace—in the exact manner of the Icarus figure adorning the band's Swan Song record label.

Also like the mythical Icarus (and the flaming Hindenburg

emblazoned on their first album cover), Zeppelin blew apart and burned out at the tippy-top of its stratospheric adventure.

But what a ramble. And what magnificent, ongoing fallout.

The musical tie between Zep and Metallica is essentially the same as that between Zep and every other band to follow in its wake, particularly in the case of monster-stomping, firestorm-guitar four-pieces: Tune down, wail hard, kill 'em all.

More direct is the Zep's showing Metallica how it's done when you not only want to be the hugest band in the universe, you want to be so huge that all that could possibly suffice is becoming your own universe, in and of yourself.

Depending on which fan of what era you ask, either "Master of Puppets" or "Enter Sandman" qualifies as the Metallica equivalent of Zeppelin's "Stairway to Heaven"—each one a self-contained mini-stadium-festival showboating the band's most potent pyrotechnics, winning hearts and minds and souls and who knows how many virginities in the course of their running times, which extended infinitely beyond just what's on the record or pouring out of the Marshall stacks onstage, echoing no less than all the way into eternity.

Led Zeppelin proved to Metallica that you can be the Beatles and the Stones—love gods and demon dogs—all at once. And you can do it on your own terms, driven by your own ambitions. Just as long as they, and you, keep it gigantic.

LYNYRD SKYNYRD

Cutting through the '70s Malibu quaalude haze of Democratic Party fund-raisers such as the Eagles and Fleetwood Mac on one coast and Springsteen and James Taylor on the other, hell-raising plane-crashers Lynyrd Skynyrd brought to classic rock a voice of the truly reviled.

Up from the swamps of the Confederacy soared these whiskey-boiled, bare-knuckled brutes who felt intense pride over their necks' crimson hue. Watergate didn't bother them. Neil Young's attempt to lecture them did. They were free as a bird, and that bird could never change. Not even in death.

In the best sense, Lynyrd Skynyrd were, as their song says,

simple men. They were driven, dedicated, antiauthoritarian, and unapologetic, whether that meant punching their way out of life-threatening scraps over their long hair growing up, or, once they became stars, directing the limousine-liberal rock establishment toward which Gulf of Mexico short pier on which they might take a long ride.

Named for their mirthless human crew-cut of a high school gym teacher, Lynyrd Skynyrd did for wild-eyed Southern boys reared on rock and country what Metallica would for punky metal burnouts everywhere a few years hence.

Their music incorporated the sounds on which they grew up, and then ran on its own energy and new ideas. Their lyrics spoke directly to—and for—the audience.

Skynyrd's triple-guitar firing squad, biker-friendly aesthetic, and booze-past-puking notion of an enjoyable night out places them sure-footedly within the boundaries of heavy metal. James Hetfield's channeling of (literally) fallen Skynyrd front man Ronnie Van Zant places the group muddy-boots-deep in the DNA of Metallica.

The importance of Skynyrd not only to Metallica but to the rest of rock is evidenced by the cover of "Tuesday's Gone" on *Garage Inc.* The track's guest players include Les Claypool of Primus, Jerry Cantrell of Alice in Chains, Pepper Keenan of Corrosion of Conformity, John Popper of Blues Traveler, and Jim Martin of Faith No More. Original Skynyrd member and "Tuesday" cowriter Gary Rossington also joins in on guitar.

The box art of the 2009 video game *Guitar Hero: Metallica* actually misspells "Lynyrd Skynyrd," dropping the final *y* so that it just reads "Lynyrd Skynrd." This typo, however mortifying at first, is now just an amusing footnote that further and more deeply connects the two bands. As does tragedy.

The classic Lynyrd Skynyrd lineup took the ultimate bum trip on October 20, 1977. The band's tour plane ran out of fuel, and the resulting crash killed Ronnie Van Zant, guitarist Steve Gaines, backup singer Cassie Gaines (Steve's sister), their road manager, and the two pilots.

The music, of course, lives on, not just in and of itself, or in covers like Metallica's "Tuesday's Gone," but in the spirit of every hard rock band since Skynyrd that hits the stage cool and cocky and greasy and gritty and doing it exactly the way they want to, consequences—and Yankee know-it-alls—be damned.

QUEEN

Hail to Queen. The pomp and circumstance of rock's most extravagantly theatrical foursome is matched (surpassed, really) only by their hugeness of their musical ideas and the technical mastery with which they brought them to everlasting life—with furious flare.

Minus the glitter and smiles and "anything (and/or anyone) goes" sexual libertinism, Metallica learned volumes from guitarist Brian May, drummer Roger Taylor, bassist John Deacon, and, needless to say, the cosmic dervish up front, Freddy Mercury.

For *Rubaiyat*, a 1988 compilation album celebrating Elektra Records' fortieth anniversary, Metallica actually had to fight to perform a Queen song. It wasn't much of a throw-down, though: Nerd-pop duo They Might Be Giants had wanted to dork up "We Will Rock You/We Are the Champions." Metallica muscled them out by insisting on their own version of "Sheer Heart Attack." The Giants squeaked away (opting instead for a more fitting Phil Ochs folk song), while Metallica wailed out one of their greatest covers, which remains a live-show highlight.

At Wembley Stadium's gargantuan 1992 Freddy Mercury tribute concert, Metallica paid homage to the AIDS-felled front man in the show's first half with a performance of "Enter Sandman," "Sad but True," and "Nothing Else Matters."

For the night's second set, whereupon Queen's surviving members took the stage, James Hetfield belted out "Sheer Heart Attack" with additional power supplied by Black Sabbath's Tony Iommi on guitar.

The glam panache of Queen and the metal-punk brusqueness of Metallica echo one another in intensity, integrity, and a singleness of purpose stated most perfectly as: "We will / We will ROCK you!"

THE ROLLING STONES

Famously touted as "The World's Greatest Rock 'n' Roll Band"—a cause for debate in some circles—the Rolling Stones are, without question, the first hard rock band to transfix and transform the entire human species and, in essence, to define what hard rock is and, more importantly, to demonstrate, as no one else ever has, what it can be.

Furthermore, once the Stones established these rules, they continued to push them and break them and redefine them and always, always stay ahead of the pack. Their innovation and longevity are testimony to the mightiness of the Stones not only in the rock pantheon, but in the very DNA of everything that defines Metallica.

Early on, Metallica expressed dismissive disdain for the yin to the Stones' yang, exemplified in 1989 by James Hetfield's telling *Rolling Stone*, "The Beatles and shit like that, I never dug so much." (Amusingly, later in the piece, Hetfield overhears a bass run from *Abbey Road* and, taken aback, says: "Hey, what's that? That's pretty fucking hot!" It's a nice demonstration of how the band always keeps its ears open.)

If young Metallica did revere the Stones, though, it was more implicit than declared outright. The classic rock–era acts that Metallica definitely did listen to and tout as their favorites—Zeppelin, Cream, Hendrix, Sabbath, Deep Purple, Alice Cooper—trace their lineage most directly to Stonesdom.

The essence of what those old gods brought to the young turks is there in the Stones' very first records and earliest public appearances: the dirty blues, the swagger, the theatrical abandon, the ramshackle rapture. And in that collision of movement and sound and style and menace arose a clarion call: "Get up now and get yer ya-ya's out!"

Of all unlikely sages, Bruce Springsteen nailed the catalytic importance of the Stones in the advent of metal and punk by explaining: "When you watched the Beatles, you knew there were only four guys in the world who could do that job, and they were onstage, doing it. But when you saw the Stones, you thought, 'Hey, maybe I could do that, too! Let me give it a shot!'"

Beyond the do-it-yourself stimulus, though, something deeper lurked within the Stones . . . something threatening . . . something upsetting . . . something heavy . . . something, in a pointedly nascent form, metal.

You can feel it in the soul-deep sinister rumblings and possessed fluidity of Keith Richards's guitar, in the electrified howls and otherworldly spasms of front man Mick Jagger, and in the under-thunder portent of a shifting rhythm section driven by drummer Charlie Watts.

It's scary and it's real. It's *not* only rock 'n' roll . . . but it is.

As they rocked and rolled on throughout the '60s, the Stones' initially implied underpinnings of darkness and damnation became overt and definitive, even—in a very real sense—dangerous.

The Stones album *Their Satanic Majesties Request* predates Black Sabbath's debut by three years. Their worldwide pop radio smash "Sympathy for the Devil" beat Sab by two years.

Most famously, just months after Jagger commingled with occultist Kenneth Anger for the film *Invocation of My Demon Brother* (1969), the Stones buried flower power once and forever at the notorious Altamont Speedway concert, where their drunken, acid-inflamed Hells Angels security force pulverized fans and musicians alike, even killing one crowd member.

So by the time Tony Iommi birthed heavy metal in 1970 with the opening three-chord "devil's note" on *Black Sabbath*, the Stones had broken fertile, unholy ground for the delivery.

That pedigree leads to 2005, when Metallica, who had been head-lining stadiums for more than a decade, proudly announced that they would be the opening act, in San Francisco, for the Rolling Stones.

In the group's official announcement, Lars Ulrich stated: "Over the course of our career we've been fortunate enough to share the stage with bands we grew up on, admired, and respected, including AC/DC, Deep Purple, Guns N' Roses, and Iron Maiden. The only band that we have never played with but have always wanted to is the Rolling Stones."

As the gigs occurred during Metallica's post–*St. Anger* downtime, Ulrich continued: "Having the opportunity to play with them in our hometown of San Francisco is both an honor and a privilege. These two shows are about nothing other than having fun and playing music . . . nothing to sell, nothing to promote, nothing to talk about . . . no fuckin' agenda at all. The is the reason we started a band twenty-five years ago, and we are psyched and appreciative of this awesome opportunity."

Their Satanic majesties made the request . . . and their metallic heirs heeded the call.

Long live goddamned rock 'n' roll.

RUSH

After Metallica's 2006 induction into the Rock and Roll Hall of Fame, Kirk Hammett knew who should go in next.

"I would have to say Rush," he said. "I think they're a great band who took rock to a different level altogether in terms of like songwriting and technical proficiency, and I believe that they deserve to be in the Hall of Fame."

That is high (and even mildly surprising) praise from the man regularly identified as the world's biggest UFO fan.

Canada's premier prog-metal power triad—vocalist Geddy Lee, guitarist Alex Lifeson, and drum deity Neil Peart—soldiers on as one of music's most polarizing forces. Worshipped by devotees, despised by critics, Rush sell out arenas. On their own terms. Always.

The musicians in Rush rank among rock's virtuosos. Peart's heady words are the lyrical equivalent of Lee's voice—they would be mortifying if they didn't work but, oh, how they do.

Rush has proven that by chasing one's muse, however off-putting, one may reap the ultimate rewards.

You can be politically incorrect—for Rush that meant dedicating *2112* to "the genius of Ayn Rand"; for Metallica it meant cutting off Napster and killing it—as long as you're true to yourself.

Occasionally, that truth results in the rapping skull in Rush's "Roll the Bones" video or Lars Ulrich's periodic flirtation with mascara . . . but so go the perils of playing for the ultimate stakes: complete artistic freedom.

Rush fights that good fight with every note. Heavily.

SIR LORD BALTIMORE

"Brooklyn, New York's Sir Lord Baltimore were arguably America's first bona fide heavy metal band," writes music historian Eduardo Rivadavia, "and the funny thing is, they didn't even know it, since the style had yet to establish itself when the band first burst onto the scene."

The borough that also gave us legendary metal club L'Amour, "where rock lives" (and where Metallica first played in 1983), and Peter Steele's two-pronged incarnation in proto-thrashers Carnivore and goth hydra Type O Negative—as well as your humble author—was the first to break heavy by way of this power trio.

In fact, *Creem* magazine scribe Mike Saunders gets credit for the debut use of the term to "heavy metal" in 1970 to describe Sir Lord Baltimore. Listen to *Kingdom Come*, the album Saunders was reviewing, and you'll grasp how he simply could not have employed any other words.

While conjuring Black Sabbath (for whom Sir Lord Baltimore would open at New York City's legendary rock concert hall, the Fillmore East), Led Zeppelin, Humble Pie, and even the Stooges, *Kingdom Come* offers a perfect take on the hard-and-heavy of the time all its own.

And, as noted, Sir Lord Baltimore is actually the common ancestor from which all American metal has descended and evolved. If you like Metallica, you owe it to yourself to listen to the moment when these pioneers walked out of the sea (at Coney Island), plugged into their Marshall stacks, and rocked the species. Forward.

STEPPENWOLF

"I like smoke and lightning / HEAVY METAL THUNDER!"

And so, with those words, Steppenwolf codified the hardest form of rock music and bestowed upon it a name that, among its innumerable other variations, would figure directly into Metallica.

The lyrics come from Steppenwolf's "Born to Be Wild," the theme song from the iconic biker film *Easy Rider* (1969) and still the unbeatable anthem for mounting a hog, gunning the motor, and tearing off into the endless horizon. Chrome, leather, noise, speed, mocking death at full throttle: "Born to Be Wild" manifests a rebel lifestyle that is literally heavy and literally metal.

Steppenwolf, however, is much more than just the one song you know by heart. The group, led by singer John Kay, scored other major hits ("Magic Carpet Ride," "Rock Me," "Move Over"), and their first two albums (*Steppenwolf* and *Steppenwolf the Second*, both released in 1968) are blues-bombing, psychedelicized, proto-metal knockouts.

As did countless other outlaw biker legends, Steppenwolf crashed fast and burned hard. But the band's legacy roars on every time a musician rides the lightning and pumps out heavy metal thunder.

Upon Metallica's 2009 induction into the Rock and Roll Hall of Fame, James Hetfield was asked who else should be included, and he said: "Motörhead, for sure, Deep Purple, Rush, Judas Priest, Iron Maiden, and stuff before that—Steppenwolf!"

Like a true nature's child.

TED NUGENT

James Hetfield started out in Metallica as a shy, reluctant pile of un-resolved anger and zero ability to translate that burning angst into palpable heat. He looked like a greasy-maned zit-potato perched atop a stickball bat. He longed desperately for someone more char-ismatic (meaning: anyone) to relieve him of front-man burdens.

In short order, though, Hetfield morphed into a brilliantly cap-tivating beast-man/beast-master, a maniacal metal god who only got more masterful as he evolved. He embodied the unprecedented power of the band behind him and the inherent caveman sex and violence of rock itself.

So what secret fun-house mirror did Hetfield step through to make this conversion? It's no secret at all. James Hetfield turned to—and in numerous ways turned into—the grand master of all serrated-edge performance madness and hard rock machismo: Ted Nugent.

Ted Nugent is a stone-cold sober voice of insanity who rages pistol-hot above and beyond his dope-and-booze-clouded peers.

He's a far-right patriot at storm in a sea of "far out, man" hop-heads and "blame America first"—ers. And he's a kill-it-yourself carnivore and pump-action gun nut amidst throngs of tofu-soaked peace-at-any-price-niks.

From his LSD-less, late-'60s, psych-garage histrionics with the Amboy Dukes ("Journey to the Center of Your Mind") to his amphetamine-free, hyper-berserk '70s solo superstardom ("Cat Scratch Fever," "Wang Dang Sweet Poontang) to his hard-ass-in-hair-band stint in Damn Yankees ("High Enough"), "the Motor City Madman" is a living, wailing, herd-slaying arsenal of clear-headed party-hearty abandon to an entire generation of contrarian fuckups turned fucker-uppers.

But, regardless of those twists and turns, Nugent's connection to Hetfield is a line as straight as a deadeye-fired crossbow arrow into the jugular of a water buffalo.

The look was one thing. Wild blonde hair-heaps launched every which way all at once, flailing about in front of a wide-eyed, tooth-baring mug bedecked with a mustache-and-beard combo befitting Yosemite Sam after he lit up and puffed on a stick of dynamite. Nugent led on this visual cue, and Hetfield kept pace.

Hetfield even hit the gym and came to ape Nugent's body type—lean but muscular, rhesus-wily but silverback strong, the obvious payoff of regular raw protein intake. That resultant physicality, which comes across on record as well as in concert, at first belonged only to Nugent. Now it belongs only to Nugent and Hetfield.

And then there's the double-barreled nature-boy-gone-ballistic motif. Since his '70s heyday, Nugent seems to have bred entire species of creatures for his own purposes of stalking, execution, and consumption.

As Hetfield matured (perhaps ironically), the pimple-puss street fighter vexation of his youth got redirected into an array of high-testosterone outdoorsman activities—including, of course, hunting. He even mans the firepower, on occasion, with Ted Nugent.

As quoted on AllMetallica.com, Hetfield once said of their shared game-bagging adventures, "Ted's pretty intense. I love hunting; I love getting away and the quiet part of it all. I think he's a little opposite of that. Whack 'em and stack 'em, ya know."

Metallica's love of Nugent extends beyond just Hetfield. Each member has singled him out, repeatedly, for praise and admiration. The band expressed how honored they were to welcome in the new millennium onstage with Nugent in his hometown by blasting through a legendary celebration at Detroit's Pontiac Silverdome.

Ted Nugent blazed the trail that Metallica could then burn to cinders and rebuild in their own image. And more than a little bit in his image, too.

THIN LIZZY

Spearheaded by flash-lancer Phil Lynott, a dusky-skinned Dubliner of half Afro-Guyanese descent, Thin Lizzy amusingly redefined the concept of "Black Irish" while amazingly redefining the power and grace of hard rock throughout their 1970s heyday.

Thin Lizzy's sound incorporates cocksure enormity, southern boogie, country slide, Celtic warmth, and a pyrotechnic multi-guitar arsenal manned by Scott Gorham and Brian Robertson and commanded, sometimes, by axe legend Gary Moore.

Lynott's lyrics and his charged but often wistful delivery tap into the romanticism of the great Irish poets (as well as contemporary countryman Van Morrison) coupled with the pungent punch of that first pint of Guinness pint when it really kicks in.

The suave and mustachioed Lynott also embraced punk at a time when top-ticket rockers shunned it in disgust and the safety-pinned troublemakers dismissed their elders as "dinosaurs." At one point, ex–Sex Pistols Steve Jones and Paul Cook even became official Thin Lizzy members!

Alas, like too many a punk, Lynott died from a drug-related illness in 1986. Thin Lizzy, in fits and starts, has continued on without him.

Anyone with an FM radio is familiar with the inescapable "Jailbreak" and "The Boys Are Back in Town" to the point that they might not notice their greatness anymore. Go beyond them into any Thin Lizzy album to hear what so transfixed the members of

Metallica that they covered the group's revved-up traditional Irish folk song "Whiskey in the Jar."

(As a weird-covers side note, Thin Lizzy anonymously performed the instrumentation on a 1972 tribute album to another of Metallica's prime motivators titled *Funky Junction Performs the Hits of Deep Purple*).

Particularly moving is a popular YouTube clip from 2006 of Metallica performing in Ireland, where they dedicate "Whiskey" to Phil Lynott and Cliff Burton.

The huge outdoor festival crowd does more than just sing along; their revelry makes them one with the band, particularly when James Hetfield switches the lyric "a cannonball roarin'" with "a Dublin roarin'."

The benediction of their fallen comrades becomes tangible; the clear (if not direct) line from Thin Lizzy to Metallica gets laid bare.

Raise your glass as you bang your head.

UFO

Kirk Hammett says his inspiration to play guitar took flight "the second he heard Michael Schenker's guitar lead on "Mother Mary" by UFO.

"Schenker wasn't playing blues-based solos," Hammett says. "He was playing modes—scales that sounded almost classical. Rhythmically, he was out the door. To this day, UFO is my favorite band in the whole world."

Launching from London in 1969, UFO initially hit big only in Japan and Germany. The latter land proved especially fruitful in 1973, after the group beamed up a native son, Michael Schenker, then of Scorpions and, at 18, a world-class guitar prodigy.

Schenker piloted UFO to global success with 1974's *Phenomenon*. Two years and two albums later, UFO additionally abducted multi-instrumentalist Paul Raymond from Savoy Brown, resulting in their best-known album, *Lights Out*.

There's a solid chance that either one of that record's two singles, "Lights Out" or "Too Hot to Handle," is playing right now on your local classic rock station.

Go check.

Was I right?

Yet, as noted, UFO's FM radio hits continue to cause speeding incidents on Midwest highways, and they function as the crucial bridge between post-'60s hard rock and the New Wave of British Heavy Metal.

Plus, UFO is Kirk Hammett's favorite band in the whole world.

VAN HALEN

For several generations (too many), the gargoyles that write professionally on rock have routinely touted a series of "game change" moments in the history of the music it's been their mission to ruin.

One maliciously excluded bomb-lobbed-at-Archduke-Ferdinand is "Eruption," the second track on the first Van Halen record, erupting (for sure) between "Runnin' with the Devil" and "You Really Got Me."

With "Eruption," Eddie Van Halen sucks in everything that Les Paul and Dick Dale and Jimi Hendrix and Jeff Beck and Jimmy Page and Tony Iommi and Ritchie Blackmore, et al, hath wrought and, with equal parts mastery and mischief, power-pukes it back out by way of a zillion new notes and a zillion new techniques in a zillion different tones and colors spraying in a zillion different directions and landing anywhere and everywhere anybody would ever again pick up an electric guitar.

So why is this transformative rapture and revelation kept out of the canon?

"Most rock critics prefer Elvis Costello to Van Halen," VH front-whirlwind David Lee Roth pointed out, "because most rock critics look like Elvis Costello."

Note, then, that Metallica, while never exactly reviled, didn't get U2-proportioned proctological tongue-baths from the rock press until the band left its barbarian locks at the barbershop.

Van Halen's first-wave steroid burlesque and follow-up decade of Hagarized synth-balladry may each seem a far cry from the bummer-embracing Metallica, but pairing these super troopers together proved monumentally successful on the 1988 Monsters of Rock Tour.

Even though they were billed second from the bottom (below Dokken, ahead of Zep-alikes Kingdom Come), Metallica ended the Monsters juggernaut ready and willing to fill stadiums on their own. Three years later, after the Black Album, they'd be able.

Much more than sharing stages and probably groupies, though, what ties Metallica to Van Halen is, once again, "Eruption."

Guitar gods had long ruled rock prior to "Eruption." But then Eddie announced, using no words whatsoever, that he was the Guitar God of Guitar Gods with a capital *G* (chord).

"Eruption" served as all future metal players' infinite code of rites, meditations, and commandments, a sonic decree from on high stating, "Aerosmith and Angus Young and Ace Frehley and the Nuge showed you one thing, and now I've shown you the rest. Be *fret*ful and multiply."

Among the immediately converted were Kirk Hammett, Dave Mustaine, and James Hetfield. Metallica most directly proceeds from New Wave of Heavy Metal and punk roots, but to really ride the lightning, they had to absorb and reinterpret the gospel of Eddie Van Halen. As did the entire rest of heavy metal, as it always will. Amen.

In 2003, *Rolling Stone* issued a list of "100 Greatest Guitarists." With publicity-generating Internet-age controversy aforethought, they ranked Eddie Van Halen at #70, two notches above Joni Mitchell (#72) but several leagues behind Thurston Moore (#34), Jack White (#17), and Kurt Cobain (#12).

Mainstream rock crit sewer-suckers (i.e., all of them) had clearly devolved since Diamond Dave's late-'70s assessment, and it's only gotten worse. They no longer throw their mollusk contrivances behind musicians that they resemble. Instead, they boost dudes who look like Joni Mitchell.

Minus the chops.

ZZ TOP

"Beer Drinkers and Hell Raisers."

That's who ZZ Top sings about. That's who ZZ Top are.

They're also a powerfully original hard rock megaforce who,

midcareer, cracked the code for pop superstardom. So when Metallica talks about ZZ Top's importance to them, it's not purely on a musical level.

But the music is nothing to sneeze (and then blow your nose into your beard) at.

Sunbaking the power-trio dynamic and juicing it with hot sauce, ZZ Top sped out of Dallas in 1970 with Billy Gibbons on guitar, Dusty Hill on bass, and Frank Beard on drums.

Gibbons and Hill sport the band's signature Cousin-Itt-length hang-down facial hair. Beard wears only a neatly trimmed mustache. Naturally.

The threesome toured constantly throughout the '70s, becoming a top-ticket arena attraction through the sheer force of their live show (particularly when they rolled out with the Stones) and a series of albums that sounded perfectly of their time and place—but didn't sound like anybody else.

They weren't southern rock or country or blues or Latin or Caribbean or soul or metal. They were all of that and more. ZZ Top were just themselves.

Nineteen seventy-three's *Tres Hombres* spawned the dirty-boogie classic "La Grange," with the '75 follow-up *Fandango!* and its Top 40 single, "Tush." By America's bicentennial, ZZ Top concerts were breaking audience attendance records set by Elvis Presley and Led Zeppelin. More hits followed, and more stadiums got turned into greasy, gritty Lone Star State roadhouses, one show and 25,000 fans at a time.

The onset of the 1980s changed everything. ZZ Top would not roll over and blow away like tumbleweeds amidst the onslaught of New Wave and MTV. Billy Gibbons, on the contrary, polished up his most pointy-toed cowboy boots and set out to kick the decade's ass. Which, via the ten-times-platinum 1983 album *Eliminator*, he did.

Gibbons studied the beat sequencing of the top pop hits of the day and systematically set out to capitalize on it. He then created *Eliminator* with a team of engineers almost entirely using synthesizers and electronic instruments. Hill and Beard got to rest up until the epic "Worldwide Texas" tour to promote the record.

MTV was crucial in fashioning ZZ Top: Mach II, as well. The beards, the sunglasses, and Gibbons's 1939 Ford Coupe (for whom *Eliminator* was named) appeared in iconic videos for "Gimme All Your Lovin'," "Sharp-Dressed Man," and "Legs." The three went from being rock stars to being an American institution.

ZZ Top's follow-up albums produced diminishing returns, but, like all post-*Thriller* Michael Jackson albums, they didn't have to compete with their makers' biggest seller. Immortality had been achieved.

Metallica frequently cites ZZ Top as one of the bands they loved most while growing up. The early commitment to unique, genre-hopping hard rock ties the two bands together, as does the eventual dead-eyed dedication to making a leap to commercial hyperspace.

GARAGE DAYS RE-REVISITED
The 1960s Garage Rock Revolution

Something wicked this way came in the mid-1960s, from basements and backyards and high school practice rooms and the crowded carports from which garage rock takes its name.

Garage rock sonically embodies the post-greaser/pre-hippie teenage zeitgeist that first pipelined in from wild-guitar surf rock, then flooded the human hive mind by way of the Beatles on *Ed Sullivan*, and finally got roughed-up and blues-blackened by the Stones.

It is raw, it is sloppy, it is primal, and it is frequently likened to sounds made by cavemen. With good reason. But garage rock is not so much uncivilized as it is pre-civilized.

Once everybody learned to play, the general consensus is that rock music got better (a frequently cited example is "I Wanna Hold Your Hand" vs. the White Album). But it's hard to argue that it was ever again as much fun (see the previous example).

Garage rock is typically aligned with punk, but it's the greasy, grimy, gutbucket birth portal of metal, too.

Classic Garage Rock Essentials

? and the Mysterians, "96 Tears"

13th Floor Elevators, "You're Gonna Miss Me"

The Amboy Dukes featuring Ted Nugent), "Journey to the
   Center of Your Mind"

The Beau Brummels, "Laugh Laugh"

The Easybeats, "Friday on My Mind"

The Electric Prunes, "I Had Too Much to Dream Last Night"

The Flamin' Groovies, "Shake Some Action"

The Kingsmen, "Louie Louie"

The Knickerbockers, "Lies"

The McCoys, "Hang on Sloopy"

The Monks, "Black Monk Time"

The Music Machine, "Talk Talk"

Paul Revere and the Raiders, "Kicks"

Them, "Gloria"

Sam the Sham and the Pharaohs, "Wooly Bully"

The Sonics, "The Witch"

The Standells, "Dirty Water"

Swingin' Medallions, "Double Shot of My Baby's Love"

The Trashmen, "Surfin' Bird"

The Wailers, "Tall Cool One"

Alice Cooper on the Billion Dollar Babies tour. (Photofest)

2

THE FRAYED ENDS OF SANITY:
CRACKPOTS AND ICONOCLASTS

It's convenient that "rock" rhymes with "shock." They go together. Volumes exist on Elvis being filmed only from the waist up on *Ed Sullivan*, Little Richard pounding piano keys with his feet while baying, "A-wop-bop-a-loo-bop-a-lop-bop-bop!" Bill Haley inciting teenage riots with "Rock Around the Clock," and the Beatles flipping wigs everywhere by way of their "long" (for 1964) hair.

The furies that liberated heavy metal originally gestated in moments like those, and the following lunatic bricklayers paved the way for Metallica to become the most popular hard rock ensemble of all time.

ALICE COOPER

In 1968, Detroit punk Vincent Furnier reinvented his garage combo—and simultaneously co-invented heavy metal—when he darkened the group's sound and changed his look to that of mascara-smeared Bette Davis in *Whatever Happened to Baby Jane?* and his identity to Alice Cooper.

Rock heroes clogged up the scene, Cooper reasoned, so now he would be the first rock villain. Needless to say, he pulled the villainy off heroically.

Combining blood-soaked, multimedia stage spectaculars with many of the most irresistible hits ever recorded, by 1974 sick and scary Alice Cooper ruled as the biggest rock phenom this side of the River Styx.

Booze and bad decisions sidelined Cooper for some time, but

his legend ascended and his influence expanded into punk, industrial, noise, and a momentary late-'80s movement combining each
of the previous called "pigfuck." (Bands playing this style of music
included Big Black, Killdozer, and Pussy Galore.)

Heavy metal, of course, reveres Cooper as an unholy god,
which he finds endlessly amusing between playing golf and playing
concerts and, yes, going to church.

ARTHUR BROWN

Alice Cooper's makeup kit is more famous, but British madman
Arthur Brown wore the colors first.

Done up in the familiar black-and-white facial schemata later
borrowed not only by Cooper, but Kiss, King Diamond, the Misfits,
Marilyn Manson, and black metal's entire "corpse paint" brigade,
he performed as the Crazy World of Arthur Brown, and belted out
wild, psychedelic caterwauls while gyrating outlandishly and wearing a metal helmet topped by an actual open flame.

Brown's big hit was "Fire," which opens with him declaring: "I
am the god of Hell-FIRE, and I give you . . . FIRE!"

Arthur Brown was a key spark in the blaze that Metallica keeps
burning.

BLUE CHEER

San Francisco power trio Blue Cheer, named for a particularly
potent strain of acid-master Owsley Stanley's stock in trade, took
the greaser snarl of Eddie Cochran's "Summertime Blues," fried it
in consciousness-altering noxiousness, cranked the amplification,
blew it up huge, and, with their hit 1968 cover, whelped the first
radio touchstone from which acid rock, heavy metal, punk, stoner
rock, and grunge could all be traced.

Vincebus Eruptum, the album that contains "Summertime," boasts
five other psychedelic flash-forwards to hard rock's future.

When you stick your head in there, you can still see forever.

BOB DYLAN

Unless you were there (and, being born in 1968, I wasn't), one can only imagine the shock of hearing Bob Dylan for the first time at the dawn of the 1960s' counterculture revolution.

The scratchy guitar, the atonal harmonica, the weird words, and, above all, that irritated-alley-cat-with-adenoids voice—somehow, all that added up to Bob Dylan, premier poet and conceptual bedrock of his, and each subsequent, generation.

As with Andy Kaufman's inexplicable "Mighty Mouse" bit on the first *Saturday Night Live*, the bewildered public simply responded with a collective "I don't know why this works, but it does!"

Thereafter, Dylan figures into the Metallica story first in what he did with lyrics—turning the personal political, and vice versa—but even more so in pursuit of his own vision, with disregard for fans' or the media's approval . . . or disapproval.

At the 1965 Newport Folk Festival, perpetually acoustic solo folkie Bob Dylan plugged in and rocked out with a fully electrified backing band. The crowd booed him off the stage.

The move incited brays of "Traitor!" among true believers in a manner not matched until Metallica's mid-'90s haircuts and softening of their sound for alt-rock radio. Balls come in endless forms, but count Bob Dylan's and Metallica's among the biggest.

FRANK ZAPPA

Misanthrope, megalomaniac, mad genius, and rock's first great, lovable a-hole, drug-shunning Frank Zappa trouser-watered flower power and lit up the Summer of Love with soberly sinister blasts of bile and grating gales of (hilarious) mean-spirited humor.

Zappa's dominant '60s outfit, the Mothers of Invention, mocked rock's sacred cows so effectively that their targets (the Beatles and Stones, in particular) could only respond with awe. And then they stole his ideas.

Throughout the '70s, Zappa's technical explorations pushed him in a metal direction, where only fret-master sidemen on the high order of Steve Vai and Joe Satriani could keep up.

Most metal of all, in 1985, Zappa marched on Capitol Hill with Dee Snider and John Denver(!) to defend W.A.S.P. and the Mentors (and you and me and Metallica) from the censorious Parents Music Resource Center.

Zappa died from prostate cancer in 1994, but he remains a hero to heshers and headbangers everywhere, a true avant-garde visionary who could connect to denim-clad dirtbags by way of heavy musical truth and brilliantly constructed diarrhea jokes.

MC5

Rolling like stones launched from combustion rockets made of chrome-plated Detroit steel, the MC5 took guerilla combat to the hairy rabble uprisings of their day, mixing real acid with the sugar cube variety, pulling the pin on their hard rock grenades, and letting fly.

Their debut album, *Kick Out the Jams*, was recorded live, as was the band's open-air Chicago performance amidst the 1968 Democratic Convention riots—FBI surveillance cameras captured the MC5's Lincoln Park concert with genuine cinematic flair (check them out in the documentary *MC5: A True Testimonial*).

Three albums and a whole heap of heroin in, the band flamed out in 1972, but what they and Detroit neighbors the Stooges started would flower a few years hence into punk rock and, with a few more detours, Metallica.

THE MONKS

Black metal begins with "Black Monk Time," the compellingly repellant, freakishly brilliant 1965 album from the Monks, a cabal of American GIs stationed in Germany who billed themselves as "the Anti-Beatles."

Clad in black robes and Friar Tuck haircuts, wearing nooses as neckties and scowls as they played, the Monks start off by babbling over a cacophonous groove about King Kong, James Bond, Vietnam, the atomic bomb, and (most importantly) Pussy Galore, and then really get on with it in demented nuggets such as "Shut Up" and "I Hate You."

I repeat: This was 1965, and these were U.S. soldiers killing time in Hamburg en route to killing and/or being killed in south-east Asia. The madness (in every sense) of these young men in that moment blasts out of every sound they made.

ROKY ERICKSON

Sunbaked and psilocybin-sautéed deep in the medulla oblongata of Texas, Rocky Erickson's killer ensemble the 13th Floor Elevators chemically invented psychedelic music on their 1966 single "You're Gonna Miss Me."

After that, there was no getting the heady "mush" out of rock's larger "room." The Elevators' devoted followers included Janis Joplin and ZZ Top's Billy Gibbons, but any dreams of larger stardom were dashed when Erickson got popped for a single joint in 1969.

His strategy to duck jail by pleading insanity proved an even harsher buzzkill, however, as Erickson spent three years enduring electroshock convulsions, Thorazine brain baths, and untold psychological savagery at the hands and devices of Texas mental "health" facilitators.

Once freed, Roky believed space creatures possessed him and even fought to be legally declared an alien.

The upside of this state-induced madness is that Roky subsequently recorded mind-blowing hard rock mini-epics on metal-friendly themes inspired by the visions of his sickness—twisting and shouting paeans to vampires, zombies, demons, alligators, atom brains, occult temples, white faces, a bloody hammer, a two-headed dog, and, everywhere, Lucifer.

SCREAMING JAY HAWKINS

Operatic Ohio blues belter Screaming Jay Hawkins created "shock rock" on his landmark 1956 howler "I Put a Spell on You" and in stage shows where he'd emerge from a coffin clad in leopard skins, wave a scepter topped by a smoking skull (named Henry), and perform voodoo whamma-jammas on all bug-eyed comers.

THE STOOGES

Nineteen seventy-seven is the officially anointed "the year that punk broke" but—even in strict terms of punk-qua-"PUNK!"—

let's remember that the first Ramones record came out in 1976, the Dictators' *Go Girl Crazy* hit in 1975, and the Stooges played their first gig on Halloween night all the way back in 1967, with their self-titled debut album pile-driving the public six months later (beginning with the song "1969"; the count-up continues . . .).

Iggy Stooge (as he was known prior to Pop), backed by the Asheton brothers (Ron on guitar, Scott on drums) and bassist Dave Alexander, charged headlong into plasma-caked and peanut-butter-smeared extremes not even the most avant-garde art forms had dared to explore. Because he had to do it.

Harder, louder, and heavier than had ever been previously imagined, the Stooges were more than musicians, more than maniacs, more than mere pioneers—they were, in fact, inventors. Because they had to do it.

"I was really determined to use the noises on myself, as if I were a scientist experimenting on himself," Pop writes in his autobiography, "like Dr. Jekyll or the Hulk." The results, for sure, were similarly monstrous.

As it was for fellow Detroit marauders the MC5, it was three albums and out for the Stooges, but their effect echoes on in every note of hard rock ever since (with the leap from the Stooges' "Search and Destroy" to Metallica's "Seek and Destroy" being one of the more obvious examples).

The Stooges are the Black Sabbath of punk rock. Because they had to be.

LEPER MESSIAH

10 Reasons Why Metallica Collaborating with Lou Reed Made Perfect Sense

*L*ulu is just that: a lulu of a record featuring what many thought to be the loony prospect of collaboration between Metallica and Lou Reed.

From the initial announcement, typical reactions to the idea of the world's most popular hard rock band and the world's most bedraggled talk-singing underground anti-superstar making beautifully ugly music together ranged from to head-scratching to hostility to ever fresher rounds of "No, seriously, is this a joke?"

Lulu, of course, proved to be no laughing matter.

Similarly serious was the kinship between the two camps, with at least one member being brave enough to invoke peas in a pod.

Metallica partnering with Lou Reed not only is less bizarre than it first seemed, but these following ten reasons may prove that it was even, like Lou's donning a long leather jacket in summertime swelter, inevitable.

1. Lou Reed Has Long Been Hailed as "the Godfather of Punk"

Nailing down who, exactly, first coined the moniker "Godfather of Punk" regarding Lou Reed is a task as foolish as the essential concept itself is credible. Because the "punk"-ness in question is all about attitude.

Lou Reed crystallized a jaded, street-hustling, bugger-'em-all demeanor that endures to this very moment.

Musically speaking, Punk Rock Lou is also not so long a stretch. Bear in mind that capital-*P* Punk very much did begin with the perversion of Lou Reed's groundbreaking art-noise cabal, the Velvet Underground.

2. The Velvet Underground Inspired Bands the Way Metallica Inspired Bands

Similarly hard to pin down is the originator of this sentiment: "The Velvet Underground may have only ever sold 10,000 records, but all 10,000 people who bought those records went on to start their own bands."

The Velvet Underground channeled a spark that inspired countless creative listeners to actively join in and extend the musical conversation.

Metallica can claim the same impetus status, in fact, millions of times over.

3. Ostrich Guitar Tuning

Metal musicians often tend to be tech geeks and giddy nerds for sonic innovation—forever bending strings, messing with tunings, and reconfiguring both instrumentation and actual instruments.

Cliff Burton, Kirk Hammett, and Dave Mustaine most assuredly fall into that class.

One of the most deceptively unshowy but profoundly expansive setup techniques has been ostrich tuning, in which a guitar's strings are all tuned to the same pitch class (most often it's D, but A#, B, and F also regularly get ostrich-ized).

The originator of ostrich guitar is Lou Reed.

Ostrich tuning remains in use today, fortifying even the simplest compositions with sweep and grandeur, two crucial metal elements if ever there were any (check out Soundgarden's all-E ostrich tuning on "Mind Riot" for an example).

4. Reed Documented Narcotics Use at a Time When Rock Only Dared to Cover Psychedelics

While the Beatles rhapsodized about "Lucy in the Sky with Diamonds" and the Stones sent up suburban pill-popping on "Mother's Little Helper," Lou Reed shot right to the main vein of the matter on the 1967 debut album *The Velvet Underground and Nico*.

First, there's "I'm Waiting for the Man," a spurts-and-all chronicle of copping dope in Harlem, followed several numbers later by seven-minute feedback-inflamed death bath titled, bluntly, "Heroin."

Those songs, along with a whip-cracking spelunk into sadomasochistic sex on "Venus in Furs," forever extended the topics and topicality that could be taken on by rock.

Even more than punk, metal has battered down the boundaries when it comes to licentious lyrics and unsanitary sentiments. And that was very directly made possible by the cultural cracks in the dams of supposed "good taste" made by the proudly damned and brazenly decadent Velvet Underground.

"Heroin" is the ungodly godfather of "Master of Puppets."

5. *Rock N Roll Animal* Is One of the Great Live Rock Albums

Backed by key members of Alice Cooper's band, Lou Reed pumped up his back catalogue with dark musical brawn and Bowie-like glitter flourishes on 1974's *Rock N Roll Animal*, one of the very greatest live albums of rock's golden age of very great live albums.

"At its best," wrote the *Village Voice's* Robert Christgau, "Reed's live music brings the Velvets into the arena in a clean redefinition of heavy, thrilling without threatening to stupefy . . . this is a live album with a reason for living."

As colossal as Metallica's 1993 boxed set *Live Shit: Binge and Purge* is, and as innovative as 1999's *S&M: Symphony and Metallica* has proven to be, the world's greatest heavy metal never delivered a simple, straight-up, '70s-style one-off live album.

Rock N Roll Animal could teach them much about how to do it right.

6. Lou Reed Was Wearing Women's Makeup and Making Out with Dudes in Public Decades Before Lars and Kirk Gave It a Shot

With *ReLoad* in 1997, Lars Ulrich and Kirk Hammett took Metallica in a direction that shocked many Metallica watchers—not the least of whom was James Hetfield—by prettying up their faces with makeup, puncturing their bodies with odd jewelry, and, at least once on camera, enjoying a slurpy, full-suck tongue kiss.

Again, it was shocking only because it involved the heretofore steadfastly butch Metallica. As far as hard-and-heavy musicians being so macho that they teeter over into homoerotic fairy-wing fluttering, Lou Reed sprinkled that particular brand of glandular pixie dust all over rock back when David Bowie still shared a name with the best maraca player in the Monkees and Vincent Damon Furnier was the proper way to address the lead singer of the band Alice Cooper.

Vintage glam rock served Lou Reed well, and it served Metallica even better, bringing with it such crucial acts as the aforementioned Bowie and Alice Cooper, along with Queen, Kiss, Sweet, Slade, Mott the Hoople, and other light-loafered offshoots of boot-stomping hard rock.

7. Lou Reed Worked with Kiss

Metallica is not—surprise, surprise—the first metal band with whom Lou Reed has collaborated. That honor goes to Kiss. And as weird as that seems, it gets even more wacko when you learn that the album upon which they co-labored was the perpetually goofed-on 1981 melon-scratcher, *Music from the Elder*.

Lou Reed cowrote two songs for Kiss's lone attempt at a rock opera/concept album, *Music from the Elder*—"Dark Light" and "Mr. Blackwell"—as well as the key line to the non-hit single "A World Without Heroes."

In the only Kiss song ever to be covered by Cher, Lou Reed is responsible for the sentiment "A world without heroes is like a world without sun."

8. Lou Plays Guitar on a Marianne Faithfull Album

Lou Reed entered 2011, the year of *Lulu*, by playing guitar on *Horses and High Heels*, an acclaimed album by legendary classic rock chanteuse Marianne Faithfull.

Faithfull sings, "Die-da-die-die-die-die / Die-die-die-die-die," on Metallica's 1997 hit "The Memory Remains."

And so—with apologies to one of the bands Lars always says his preppy high school classmates mistook for "heavy metal" (and it ain't REO Speedwagon)—the wheel in the sky keeps on turnin'.

9. Metallica Backed Up Reed at Madison Square Garden in 2009

During the Rock and Roll Hall of Fame twentieth-anniversary concert, Lou Reed joined Metallica onstage at Madison Square Garden to tear through the Velvet Underground's "Sweet Jane."

Metallica, reinvigorated by *Death Magnetic*, enlivened the song with rip-roaring energy. Kirk's solo breaks were especially inspired, and the effect is clear as Lou bounces and bops along.

Watch the performance on YouTube and you'll see the vivacity that continued on even offstage, where Lou proposed that they work together on something new.

Ergo, *Lulu* rocks among us.

10. *Metal Machine Music* Is the Ultimate (Literal) Sonic Embodiment of Heavy Metal

In July 1975, Lou Reed finished out his record contract with the double album *Metal Machine Music*.

It is four sides of just that: electronic hissing, feedback, static, screeches, pops, crashes, and all other stamina-smashing incarnations of amplified cacophony.

MMM announced on its shrink-wrap, "Contains No Songs," and, responding to whatever apologists attempted to assign structure and meaning to the racket (in every sense) contained therein, Reed has simply said: "Well, anyone who gets to side four is dumber than I am."

Metallica plugged into and propelled heavy metal farther and higher than anyone else ever has. *Metal Machine Music* does that too—only literally.

Dumbness is only in the ear of the beholder.

The original Motörhead. (Photofest)

3

METAL MILITIA:
EUROPE RISES ON THE NEW WAVE
OF BRITISH HEAVY METAL

Was there an "Old Wave of British Heavy Metal"? Certainly there was the heaviness and metallic elements connecting Black Sabbath, Led Zeppelin, Deep Purple, et al, but the hard rock of the first generation never seemed quite so cohesive a union.

Perhaps that's why, when punk hit circa 1977, it looked as though perhaps whatever wave upon which metal had been cresting had crashed, and it was headed out in a hurry on a tide of oblivion.

Alas, metalheads got punk's lessons through their thick hairdos and they won out. The New Wave of British Heavy Metal (NWOBHM) resulted in bands concentrating their attacks into short bursts of brawling energy on records that were created and marketed by the artists, then traded and talked up among fans and in fanzines.

"Metal played with punk attitude" is the go-to summation of the New Wave of British Heavy Metal—and also Metallica.

ANGEL WITCH

Spreading their black wings early and flapping fast to the head of the New Wave of British Heavy Metal, Angel Witch may have, alas, floated too high and too fast.

After several years of fits and starts, crashes and stoppages, Angel Witch delivered a single classic album, 1980's self-titled *Angel Witch*. It took them five years to pump out a follow-up. But as the band repeatedly fumbled, its reputation as a NWOBHM touchstone continued to grow.

Angel Witch appeals to fans of all stripes of metal who picked up on not only the band's speed and intensity, but also its unusual focus on the art of songcraft.

Lead singer and guitarist Kevin Heybourne may have been wailing about gorgons and devil's towers, but he did so via brilliant musical constructions on par with the very best pop music.

If you've ever longed to hear the pummel of Black Sabbath, the charge of Motörhead, and the groove of Aerosmith perfectly married to the catchiness of Sweet and (do I dare write this?) the Bay City Rollers, listen to Angel Witch.

Metallica certainly did.

BLITZKRIEG

Cited often by Lars Ulrich as revered forefathers, the band named for the Nazi "lightning war" was so taken by that perfect summation of their sound that Blitzkrieg had to name their flagship single—what else?—"Blitzkrieg."

Shunning any Ramones-style "Bop" and/or Sweet's "Ballroom"—although not absolutely—this "Blitzkrieg" sounds close enough to the 1971 yodel-prog head-scratcher "Hocus Pocus" by Focus to qualify as a near cover, but it radiates an energy that could only be of its time, which is to say early-'80s London, which is to say "New Wave of British Heavy Metal."

Metallica paired "Blitzkrieg" with Diamond Head's "Am I Evil"? as the B side of the title single on the 1984 *Creeping Death* EP. That combo is, as the kids say, the bomb.

And in whatever form it takes—be it by Blitzkrieg, by Metallica or, for that matter, as "Hocus Pocus" by Focus—"Blitzkrieg" is a bunker buster supreme.

BUDGIE

Wails from Wales. That's the sound of Welsh metal forebears Budgie, storm gods of the loudest order who purposefully named themselves after a breed of adorably chirpy house bird.

"I loved the idea of playing noisy, heavy rock," explains vocalist Burke Shelley of the ironic moniker, "but calling ourselves after something diametrically opposed to that."

Titlewise, Budgie was more straightforward, with albums such as *In for the Kill* and *Bandolier* (and, okay, two titter-inducers titled *Squawk* and *Impeckable*), as well as songs such as "Nude Disintegrating Parachuting Woman," "Homicidal Suicidal," "Hot as a Docker's Armpit," and "Crash Course in Brain Surgery."

It was Budgie, in fact, that caught Dave Mustaine's eye when he was perusing Lars Ulrich's 1981 classified ad looking for a guitarist. The ad also mentioned Iron Maiden—but Budgie! This guy, Mustaine had to meet. And he did.

Metallica covered "Crash Course" on the 1987 *Garage Days Re-Revisited* EP. A year later, they issued their version of Budgie's "Breadfan" as the B side of the "Eye of the Beholder" single. They also performed it as a show-closing encore on the . . . *And Justice for All* tour.

"Crash Course in Brain Surgery" so befits Metallica on so many levels that it's the subtitle of a 2007 book by culture theorist William Irwin called *Metallica and Philosophy*.

The original clocks in at a punkish two-minutes, thirty-five seconds (Metallica stretches it out another forty seconds by adding a guitar solo), while the words detail paranoia and madness atop curling riffs and bone-rumbling percussion. Budgie's Shelley sings like Robert Plant. James Hetfield just sings like James Hetfield. The connection is clear though: This is crazy rock for crazy people.

And it rocks like crazy.

CELTIC FROST

Until there was Celtic Frost, no other band sounded like Celtic Frost. In the aftermath of Celtic Frost, many other bands sounded like Celtic Frost. That's just one thing these Swiss ice-dragons share in common with Metallica.

Even the band whose hot ashes from which Celtic Frost emerged, Hellhammer, is sonically distinct from what this wildfire would ultimately blaze up to become.

Formed by singer/guitarist Thomas Gabriel Fischer—aka Tom G. Warrior—Hellhammer debuted shortly after Metallica. Whereas Metallica's *Kill 'Em All* immediately impacted all aspects of American hard rock, Hellhammer's shockingly lo-fi, deep-impact demo *Apocalyptic Raids* sparked the very specific inferno that would blaze across Europe into black metal and death metal.

Hellhammer produced six songs that shook to life a very dark and diabolical world. Renowned drummer Jan Axel Blomberg, skins-pounder for evil Swedes Mayhem, was so awestruck he simply renamed himself after the band. He became "Hellhammer." This is a move akin to, say, Iced Earth's Richard Christy telling everyone to just call him Metallica twenty years ago and having it stick.

Although he's since come to embrace Hellhammer, Tom G. Warrior pretty quickly felt constricted by its primitive attack and concocted the more wide-reaching (to say the least) Celtic Frost. As Warrior himself put it, he needed a new vehicle once he had "really learned how to play the guitar."

Bubbling among the same caustic springs as Norseman neighbors Bathory and Mercyful Fate, Celtic Frost's metal remained suitably blackened, but what was once undiluted savagery now branched out to incorporate goth, crust punk, and the new sounds thrashing about over in the states.

"Metallica, Slayer, Anthrax, the new movement of U.S. metal, had begun to dominate the scene," said Celtic Frost bassist Martin Ain, "and it was a huge stimulus."

Celtic Frost parted ways from the jeans-and-sneakers thrash scene in one immediately distinguishable way: They took Kiss's makeup and Judas Priest's leather-and-studs aesthetic to new extremes, donning furs, swords, bone jewelry, and white-faced "corpse paint." But they did so in a manner that let fans know this was no mere game of "dress-up." You can definitely hear it in the music.

At AllMusic.com, Eduardo Rivadavia describes Celtic Frost's first three albums as "the musical *Lord of the Rings* for hundreds of European kids that ended up in black metal bands of their own" (he thereby likens Hellhammer to *LOTR* precursor *The Hobbit*). And what a trilogy it is.

Morbid Tales, Celtic Frost's debut, is as heavy as the loudest bands of the day while whipping up a fantasy world devoid of Satan-chanting cliché.

The follow-up, 1985's *To Mega Therion*—Greek for "the Big Beast"—came in a cover adorned by painter H. R. Giger's rendering of the titular behemoth taking aim with Jesus slingshot (right at you!), and the sounds surpassed even that immediate attention grabber.

To Mega Therion is a huge record. It moans and grumbles on a scope that batters planets off course. To call the album monstrous would be a spot-on compliment.

Into the Pandemonium, from 1987, continued Frost's hot streak. Industrial sounds and a head-scratching headbanger cover of "Mexican Radio" by Wall of Voodoo invited the term "avant-garde metal" to the band. It fit.

Then came *Cold Lake*. Whereas it took Metallica five albums to release an album that enraged admirers, Celtic Frost got there in four.

Cold Lake is a pop-metal screwball pitched straight from the hair-hopping Sunset Strip sound. As interesting as it might seem to have the world's heaviest, strangest European metal mind attempting to wedge a place for himself between Poison and Ugly Kid Joe, it was not. The results and reaction were suitably poisonous and ugly.

Shaken to the core by *Cold Lake*'s misfire, Warrior welcomed Ain back to Celtic Frost for 1990's *Vanity/Nemesis*, a record so thrashy that it comes off as an apology.

Thirteen years and another breakup passed before Celtic Frost released the astonishing *Monotheist* in 2006. It's one of the best metal albums of the decade; so good, in fact, that it practically insured that Warrior and Ain would have to disband again. Which they did.

Whatever the future holds, Celtic Frost has earned its place among the Catacomb of Greats. They have set so many followers, for so long, down the paths they cleared that the new bands might not even know the source of what they're doing. On one hand, that's a shame. But on another, that's the price of being a true original.

DEF LEPPARD

For the uninitiated, it's discombobulating to see Def Leppard listed among the prime movers of the New Wave of British Heavy Metal. After all, you don't see Duran Duran and Culture Club ranked alongside Saxon and Iron Maiden, do you?

Alas, the glammy MTV strutters of "Pour Some Sugar on Me" represent just one aspect of Def Leppard (the one that made all the money). Early on, Lep went leather-to-leather with NWOBHM's fiercest.

Founded by bassist Rick Savage in angry response to 1977 punk, Def Leppard (note how the spelling echoes Led Zeppelin) began life as Atomic Mass. Singer Joe Elliot initially auditioned on lead guitar. Phil Collen handled axe duties. Rick Allen put his (then existing) two arms to work on the drums.

By 1979—"when the dam began to burst," as Saxon sings it— Def Leppard had roared to the forefront of NWOBHM. In fact, so primed to move was the group that, despite the omnipresence of the Union Jack in their imagery, the eye of the Leppard rested clearly on intercontinental conquest. Case in point: The second track on the band's first album, *On Through the Night*, is titled "Hello America."

On the follow-up, *High 'n' Dry*, Def Lep set a template that Metallica mined for cosmic success: They reached out to studio yogi Robert John "Mutt" Lange.

Lange was fresh off *Back in Black* by AC/DC, when he took on Lep's *High 'n' Dry*. As he had with Foreigner's monstrous *4* album a year earlier, the producer tapped brilliantly into pop platinum buried within Leppard's metal. Nowhere is this better demonstrated than on "Bringin' on the Heartache"—a swelling, sweeping, high-sheen rock baroque in 45 rpm that pushed Def Leppard to the brink of superstardom.

Leppard and Lange's next collaboration, 1984's *Pyromania*, pushed them right over that brink. *Hysteria*, in 1987, made their partnership an institution.

Following 1988's . . . *And Justice for All*, Metallica yearned for a Def Leppard–esque dominion.

In search of their own Mutt Lange, Metallica turned to Bob Rock, an engineer for '80s hard rock chart-toppers such as Bon Jovi and Loverboy, in addition to Aerosmith's comeback, *Permanent Vacation*, and Mötley Crüe's *Dr. Feelgood*.

Bob Rock helmed and honed *Metallica* (aka the Black Album) in 1991 to sales of 15 million. The band stuck with Rock for their next decade of projects, even employing him on bass for *St. Anger*, following Jason Newsted's departure.

What Mutt Lange had done for Def Leppard, Bob Rock indeed did for Metallica, only many multimillion times over.

The little girls understood. So did lots of accountants.

DIAMOND HEAD

"We're always going to be tied in as an influence on Metallica," Diamond Head guitarist Brian Tatler told *Decibel* magazine. "You never see a write up on Diamond Head without Metallica being mentioned. You can't get away from it."

Bassist Colin Kimberley concurs: "If it hadn't been for Metallica . . . we would have just been another band that was around twenty-odd years ago and disappeared."

Lars Ulrich, in turn, credits this particular New Wave of British Heavy Metal battalion with saving his life—in addition to saving and invigorating his raggedy partnership with James Hetfield back in early-'80s Los Angeles.

Each musician speaks these truths in gratitude, while feeling proud, justly, that Metallica fans who seek out Diamond Head never emerge disappointed. How could they? Metallica has been covering Diamond Head songs since before they were even Metallica.

The earliest Metallica performances, in fact, consisted of nothing *but* Diamond Head songs—most emphatically: "Am I Evil?," "Helpless," "The Prince," and "Sucking My Love"—each of which Metallica eventually recorded.

"There was something special about Diamond Head," Lars Ulrich never fails to reiterate, "no doubt about it."

Emerging in 1979 from England's terrifically metal-sounding Stourbridge area, the original Diamond Head lineup consists of vocalist Sam Harris (not the 1984 *Star Search* winner, rest assured) and drummer Duncan Scott, in addition to the aforementioned Tatler and Kimberley. They took their name from the title of a 1975 solo album by Roxy Music guitarist Phil Manzanera.

Self-recorded demo tapes alone snared Diamond Head gigs opening for AC/DC and Iron Maiden, yet yielded no major-label courtship. The solution? Cop a cue from punk and do it yourself: In 1980, Diamond Head issued "Sweet and Innocent" b/w "Streets of Gold" on indie imprint Media Records, then followed with "Shoot Out the Lights" b/w "Helpless" on their own label, Happy Face.

Shortly thereafter, Diamond Head released their first full-length album, an officially untitled long-player that's come to be known as Lightning to the Nations. In total, only two thousand copies of the record were ever printed, the first thousand of which were each signed by an individual band member, making them all-time Unholy Grails for record collectors.

Among the mavens who ordered from that first batch was seventeen-year-old Ulrich, whose LP came graced with the signature of front man Harris.

This prompted Lars to contact Diamond Head's manager, Linda Harris (yes, the singer's mom) and, in short order, to just show up at her house, prepared to aid in Diamond Head's world conquest however possible.

"It was the summer of '81," Lars told Australian rock site Triplem.com.au. "I'd been trying to get a band off the ground, [but] I got fed up with the whole thing. [So I took off overseas] to see Diamond Head who were my favorite band. I went and brownnosed my way backstage and met them."

Lars spent the hot season crashing on floors at the Harris home and tooling about England with (and without) the band. He met and pressed the flesh with Motörhead, Iron Maiden, and other key bangers of British metal. When he returned that fall to California—loaded with countless exotic records, tapes, and fanzines—Lars got James to join him in getting serious about the project they eventually deemed Metallica.

The boys got so serious, in fact, that, when confronted with Hetfield's initial shortcomings on vocals, legend has it that the young Metallicans offered the slot to Sam Harris, who responded with a thanks-but-no-thanks.

At every stage, Metallica has always acknowledged and championed Diamond Head. Ulrich produced an anthology in 1987 and the entire band encouraged a 1993 DH reunion album, *Death and Progress*, guest contributors to which include Dave Mustaine and Black Sabbath's Tony Iommi.

Diamond Head has performed and recorded sporadically in the ensuing years, with members occasionally joining Metallica onstage. Those live jams never sound like anything less than a naturally perfect fit.

It would be hard for them not to, as to listen to Diamond Head is too hear, loud and clear, so much of what awed Metallica and what they subsequently absorbed.

The music of Diamond Head is locomotive, lead-guitar-driven swagger. It's melodic but jagged and always charging. More than occasionally, Harris's voice sounds like Glenn Danzig's (or perhaps it is Danzig who sounds like Harris), thereby fusing Diamond Head to Metallica's second-most-covered favorites, the Misfits.

The connecting bond from Diamond Head's introductory number, "Shoot Out the Lights," to the first track on the first Metallica record, "Hit the Lights," is short, strong, brutal, and indelible.

Would there be a Metallica had there been no Diamond Head? Maybe. But there's no telling what it would sound like.

HOLOCAUST

Playing prog-metal arising from the realm of bagpipes, haggis, and *Braveheart*, Scotland's Holocaust made good on their name—meaning, literally, "complete destruction, especially by fire"—in their approach to hard rock. The surveyed the rules and torched them to molecules.

No song makes a better case in point than the seven-minute "The Small Hours," a steady-building spook tunnel that rolls into Celtic Frost intensity and then keeps going. And going.

"The Small Hours" was a perfect fit for Metallica's *Garage Days Re-Revisited* EP, sandwiched between covers of New Wave of British Heavy Metal titans Diamond Head and industrial punks Killing Joke.

The song is also—in its studied, deliberate, change-in-a-blink structure—a boilerplate for twisting Metallica epics from "One" to "The God That Failed" to "The Judas Kiss."

This is one Holocaust that's fun to never forget.

IRON MAIDEN

Popular consensus on heavy metal history posits that Black Sabbath invented the genre, Judas Priest codified it, and then Iron Maiden . . . well, if they didn't perfect heavy metal, they certainly did break the most direct ground from which Metallica would emerge, knife-first, full thrust, and up out of the toilet, as depicted on the (hardly) discarded cover image of *Metal Up Your Ass*.

The (damaged) brainchild of bassist and songwriter Steve Harris, Iron Maiden announced a new dawn of metal with their self-titled debut album in 1980: It was street tough, faster than the speed of punk and, unto itself, an entire self-contained universe of Iron Maidenosity.

From 1981's *Killers* onward, Iron Maiden defined itself visually through its mascot, Eddie the Head, a skinless undead mayhem-maker (first drawn by Derek Riggs as a punk rocker) who ghoulishly personifies the music's surging power, the lyrics' lurid horror, and the band's cheeky gumption.

Aside from Harris, Eddie has been Iron Maiden's one signature constant. Original singer Paul Di'Anno, a short-haired, appealingly thuggish bruiser with punkish technique, was replaced by the more swaggering and opera-prone Bruce Dickinson (pilfered from fellow NWOBHMers Samson) for *Number of the Beast* in 1982, Maiden's commercial door-kicker-inner. Other players have come and gone (and sometimes come back). But what never changes is that every iota that Iron Maiden radiates is, unmistakably, Iron Maiden.

Metallica, by mere virtue of being a metal band, owes Iron

Maiden big time. In terms of sound and tempo, the debt is clear, but even more than that, Iron Maiden demonstrated a creative integrity that Metallica would hold fast to on its first four albums: Drop a needle anywhere on any one of them and what you'll hear can only be Metallica. The same goes for the design elements of their record jackets, tour books, and T-shirts.

The message Iron Maiden imparted to Metallica and that Metallica, by extension, continues to impart to its fans is this: Know yourself. Be yourself. Push yourself. All the way. Every time. And the world will be yours.

Just look at Eddie. If you're reading this book, there's a good chance that, at any given moment, you'll see him within twenty feet of you—be it on a T-shirt, a poster, a CD cover, specialty Vans sneakers, or you name it.

That should tell you something. Something awesome.

JUDAS PRIEST

Likened by Iron Maiden vocalist Bruce Dickinson to a "mechanized Panzer attack," Judas Priest launched its blitzkrieg from Birmingham, UK, the same industrial smelting pot from which half of Led Zeppelin (Plant and Bonzo) and all of Black Sabbath poured forth.

"The thump-thump-thump, the thud-thud-thud of the stamping presses," singer Rob Halford said of the area's dreary factories and steel mills in the documentary *Heavy: The Story of Metal*, "was obviously having some kind of deep psychological effect."

"Subconsciously, that's pounded into you," adds guitarist Glenn Tipton. "We really had no choice but to play heavy metal, I think."

Whereas Sabbath invented metal in 1970, Priest perfected it over the course of the next decade.

"If you go back and you listen to some of those early Zeppelin records," points out Dee Snider in *Heavy*, "they would have bluegrass songs or madrigal tunes. Judas Priest just said, 'Nyah! That's not heavy!'"

Anthrax's Scott Ian concludes the documentary segment by declaring: "They were the first ones that were all metal all the time."

Thus, Metallica's connection to Judas Priest is direct and immediate, but not entirely obvious.

For beneath the rage and speed of both bands, in the place that immediately separated them on impact from their respective hard rock herds, is authentic emotion, eloquently voiced.

Anger, hatred, fear, and even joy—metal has never has never had a problem conjuring or conveying any of those feelings. What Judas Priest taught Metallica how to express was the infinitely more uncomfortable state of sadness.

Even at their most furious, James Hetfield's snarls can transmit frustration, confusion, isolation, and self-doubt. The pathos of Judas Priest is even more musically palpable. Just listen to the pre-chorus bridge of "Some Heads Are Gonna Roll."

It's heartbreaking. The band's upward build, with suspenseful pauses like steps on a staircase, brilliantly compounds the plaintiveness. Judas Priest's second album is named *Sad Wings of Destiny*. It's perfect.

Metallica, creators of "Harvester of Sorrow," "Bleeding Me," and "Sad but True," were baptized by those very teardrops of British steel.

MERCYFUL FATE

The Misfits got a two-song cover medley on Metallica's 1987 *Garage Days Re-Revisited* EP ("Last Caress/Green Hell"), whereas on the 1998 covers compilation, *Garage Inc.*, Metallica gives the medley treatment to no fewer than five (count 'em) numbers by mad Danish metal barons Mercyful Fate.

The titles alone indicate much of the Mercyful Fate mystique: "Satan's Fall," "Curse of the Pharaohs," "A Corpse Without Soul," "Into the Coven," and, simply, "Evil."

Mythmaking was Mercyful Fate's mastered domain, from their galloping rhythms and mystical imagery, to face-painted vocalist King Diamond's positively bizarre employment of his operatic range, to the eloquently mysterious title of their first full-length album, *Melissa* (only the last line of the nearly seven-minute title track, the record's last song, reveals Melissa to be a witch burned at the stake).

Mercyful Fate took flight at the (upside-down) crossroads of traditional heavy metal (Sabbath and Zeppelin) and power metal (Priest and Maiden), turbo-boosted by the fast-rising (or is that downward-spiraling?) black metal movement, and draped in a magisterial theatricality.

After 1984's *Don't Break the Oath*, another instant classic, Mercyful Fate disbanded.

King Diamond launched a successful solo career that continues today.

Diamond also appeared, hilariously, alongside Ozzy Osbourne on Geraldo Rivera's 1988 TV special *Devil Worship: Exposing Satan's Underground*—which may have turned more impressionable American youth onto heavy metal than the entire run of *Headbangers Ball*. T-shirts bearing his white-caked Antichrist face have remained a staple of bong dispensaries and tattoo parlors ever since.

Sensing a metallic rebirth arising in 1992, Mercyful Fate regrouped for a fruitful run until the end of the decade. They've remained on hiatus since then.

For Metallica, Mercyful Fate's immediate intensity and cross-pollination of styles made them kindred (damned) souls. The specific connection between the band and Lars Ulrich extends beyond music and philosophy into the fact that they're all from Denmark.

During his frantic fanboy days before Metallica, King Diamond was one of the metal gods with whom Lars made it a point to press the flesh. By the time *Kill 'Em All* had hit, then, the two were close. Their friendship led to one of Metallica's most legendary pranks among its own.

In 1983, King Diamond invited Metallica onstage at a Mercyful Fate show. Kirk Hammett, drunk and rocking in the worst way, leaned too hard on the singer. The next thing King Diamond remembers, he says, was being flat on his ass onstage. While the King laughed it off, the other members of Metallica insisted he was livid. For the next sixteen years, it upset Hammett (because, really, who knows what kind of curse King Diamond could lay on you?) until 1999, when he finally approached King Diamond to sheepishly apologize. And then everybody busted a gut.

Some things really are funny as hell.

MOTÖRHEAD

Propulsion. That's the word. That's what immediately set Motörhead apart from all other previous metal and punk bands—all other rock bands, period.

Derived from the Latin words *pro*, meaning "forward," and *pellere*, meaning "to drive," propulsion is what happens every time head Motörhead maven Lemmy Kilmister plunks his bass and launches this legendary British power trio (with a rotating drum and guitar contingent) upward and outward, over the top, and into your face.

Motörhead first rose, phoenixlike, out of Lemmy's 1975 firing from space-rockers Hawkwind ("for doing the wrong drugs," he claims in his self-titled documentary), and was originally to be called Bastard. Considering the commercial limitations such a named would engender, Lemmy opted instead for Motörhead, an American slang term for an amphetamine enthusiast.

Genre-busters from the git-go, Motörhead recorded under the tutelage of pub-rock legend Dave Edmunds and issued albums on New Wave–heavy Stiff Records (Nick Lowe, Elvis Costello), while hurling Sabbath-glop skyward on the wings of Sex Pistols fury. There would be no New Wave of Heavy Metal without them.

All of England's late-'70s musical subcultures embraced Motörhead, much the way skaters, skinheads, hardcore punks, and traditional metal longhairs would each hear Metallica's *Kill 'Em All* a half-decade hence and think: "All RIGHT! Finally, something just for ME!"

With his towering physique, super-Fu mustache, bulbous facial warts, and ass-length, oil-slick hair, Lemmy may well have been a natural-born icon without ever having opened his mouth. But open his mouth he did, and out erupted this tobacco-hammered whisky-rasp dragon-barf, permanently sealing his place in the pantheon of rock's most monumental practitioners of the philosophy: "Live fast, never die, just always be a good-looking corpse."

Motörhead touched each member of Metallica profoundly, so much so in the case of teenage Lars Ulrich that the boy traveled from L.A. to England in 1981 in large part just to sniff their leathers in person.

Lars also once tried to keep up with Lemmy drink-for-drink. The result was Lars passed out and covered with puke, as immortalized in a photograph inside the next Motörhead album.

After years of mutual respect (and associated ball-busting), Metallica stormed the stage at Lemmy's fiftieth-birthday party December 14, 1995, at L.A.'s Whisky A Go Go.

As "the Lemmys," in full Kilmister drag (albeit with tattoos amusingly drawn on the wrong arm), the band tore through a set of Motörhead covers. Four of the numbers they performed—"Damage Case," "Overkill," "Stone Dead Forever," and "Too Late Too Late"—were recorded as B sides for Metallica's "Hero of the Day" single, and later appeared on *Garage Inc.*

The following year, Lemmy joined Metallica in concert on James Hetfield's birthday to belt out "Overkill."

Although the only band Motörhead every name-checked with a song title is the Ramones (another Metallica favorite), perhaps no band has meant more to Lemmy and company than Metallica.

And vice versa.

RAVEN

There's no questioning the high perch of Raven in the New Wave of British Heavy Metal, nor their impact on thrash (and even hair) metal, but these Newcastle knockabouts prefer to describe their rousing music as "athletic rock." They even used to wear (and use) sports equipment in concert.

Chief among their cheerleaders has always been Metallica. Really though, the two bands have always played on the same team.

After Raven built momentum in England at both metal and punk venues, Megaforce Records founder Jon Zazula (aka Jonny Z) brought the Brits to New Jersey for a series of hugely successful performances.

Upon the release of Metallica's *Kill 'Em All* and Raven's *All for*

One, Jonny Z then teamed the groups together for the 1983 "Kill 'Em All for One" tour (often with Anthrax for support). This was Metallica's first major undertaking on the road. It agreed with them.

Come 1985, Raven scored an MTV hit with "On and On" a typically stomping rave-up whose video popped with spandex-encased metal babes. Metallica never exactly followed that route (although good luck counting up how many bands did), but it proved that even the most marginalized metal might find a way into prime time.

That would agree with Metallica, too.

SAMSON

Feeling metal course through his being and almost—but not quite—his moniker, guitarist Paul Sanson properly aligned the entire package by swapping out that first *n* in his surname for an *m*.

Thereby, the newly christened Paul SAMSON could instantly invoke the mighty-maned ass-bone-wielding ass-beater of the Old Testament and simply name his pounding, bluesy, very-late-'70s hard rock outfit after himself: Samson.

Adding to Samson's biblically proportioned potency was drummer Thunderstick, who concealed his kisser behind a head-covering known in post-*Pulp-Fiction* times as a "gimp" mask, along with front-belter Bruce Bruce, a howler given to animal-skin attire and operatic abandon (Mr. Bruce was singing under a metallization of his birth identity, with which you may be familiar: Bruce Dickinson).

In three crucial years for the New Wave of British Heavy Metal, Samson brought forth three solid albums—*Survivors* (1979), *Head On* (1980), and *Shock Tactics* (1981)— in addition to starring in a fifteen-minute short film directed by Julien Temple, *Biceps of Steel* (1980).

Come '82, though, Bruce Bruce went back to being Bruce Dickinson and departed to sing lead for Iron Maiden—a particularly stinging move, as Maiden had swiped Samson's original drummer, Clive Burr, several years earlier (Burr would later return to Samson).

Samson replaced Bruce with Nicky Moore and the group pressed on for the remainder of the decade, followed by occasional reunions through the early twenty-first century.

Horror movie fans can also enjoy glimpses of Temple's long-lost *Biceps of Steel*, as Samson performance clips from it turn up in *The Incubus* (1982), a grisly cult curiosity that centers on demon sperm.

Lars Ulrich and James Hetfield speak only with the deepest affection for Samson. There's no word on how fright-film fanatic Kirk Hammett feels about *The Incubus*, though.

SAVAGE

Mansfield, UK, outfit Savage walloped with severity at the swelling point of the New Wave of British Heavy Metal, creating at least one song so perfect—"Let It Loose"—that Metallica tried to pass it off as their own.

Just listen to it, along with the rest of Savage's classic 1983 LP *Loose N Lethal* and you'll wish it was yours, too.

Savage actually formed in 1976, comprised of teenagers Dave Menegaux (bass), Kevin Osborn (vocals and guitar), Mark Clese (lead guitar), and Gregg "Slammer" Hammer (with that name doing I even need to write "drummer"?). One disastrous gig later, the band split up, grew up, got awesome, and reunited in 1980.

Their influence on thrash is unmistakable and, in the case of Metallica, tangible, as the band routinely performed "Let It Loose" in their earliest lives sets in the hope that the audience would think it was an original.

Whether or not the ruse worked didn't matter: The song rocked—so much so, in fact, that "Let It Loose" was one of the songs Metallica included on the initial demo that landed them a gig (their second ever) opening for NWOBHM godfathers Saxon.

Not long after, Metallica took Savage out on tour in 1984. Payback isn't always a bitch.

SAXON

"Where were you in '79 when the dam began to burst?"

So ask Saxon in 1982's "Denim and Leather," their instantly immortal tribute to/summation of the dawn of the New Wave of British Heavy Metal.

Among those who could answer an emphatic "Hell, yeah!" to those and all the other queries posed by the song (e.g., "Did you read the music paper from the back and to the front?" . . . "Did you hang around your local record store?". . . "Do you dream of playing guitar or smashing up the drums"?) were ground-zero Saxon fanatics Dave Mustaine and Lars Ulrich.

The entire band could also respond, if queried as to who inspired their early penchant for spandex pants: Saxon singer Biff Byford ("You could show off your package," James Hetfield later told *Playboy*. "Wear spandex, dude. It gets you chicks!").

Beyond just music and culture, however, Saxon directly impacted on Metallica in a very real sense in 1982. The second and third public Metallica performances *ever* occurred at L.A.'s famous Whisky A Go Go. The fledgling thrashers played a pair of sets open for Saxon.

Metallica didn't get to meet the headliners that night, but they netted them $16 (a full dollar more than their previous gig) and scored their first mainstream review: "Saxon could use a fast, hot guitar player of the Eddie Van Halen ilk," wrote Terry Atkinson in the *L.A. Times*. "Opening quartet Metallica had one [in Dave Mustaine], but little else."

They would, in fact, show him (and, well, Dave Mustaine, too).

In a broader sense, what Saxon gave to Metallica is also what the band gave to the world: an unbridled love for heavy metal. Not only are "Motorcycle Man," "Stallions of the Highway," "Street Fighting Gang," and "To Hell and Back Again" typical Saxon songs—to say nothing, of course, of "Heavy Metal Thunder" and "Denim and Leather"—but the music more than matches the promise of those titles.

The Saxon sound is driving. It boogies. It pummels. It is metal that moves.

In 2010, vocalist Byford campaigned for his fellow countrymen (Saxons, indeed) to declare "heavy metal" as their religion in the UK 2011 census.

Few could proselytize more powerfully on behalf of that cause than Metallica.

SCORPIONS

At seventeen, Hannover, Germany, native Rudolf Schenker formed Scorpions (there's no "the," it's just "Scorpions"). It was 1965. How about that *scheisse?*

Well-scrubbed and fleet-fingered, the garage-rock-era Scorpions plugged into the skanky blues rumble of the Yardbirds and the Pretty Things, bolstered to no end by Rudolf's kid brother Michael Schenker on lead guitar and testosteronic tenor Klaus Meine on vocals.

By their 1970 debut, *Lonesome Crow*, Scorpions had incorporated prog fog and Zep pep, landing them a slot opening for UFO. The headliners were so impressed, they beamed Michael Schenker onboard their own craft and zoomed off to rock star heaven.

In time, though, Scorpions would greatly outpace UFO, becoming the most popular non-British metal band in Europe, and one of the world's most beloved hard rock acts, period.

You know the blockbusters: "Rock You like a Hurricane," "Big City Nights," "No One Like You," and "Still Loving You." If you are of a certain vintage you remember the raucous videos in non-stop rotation—the leather, the studs, Rudolf's defiant mustache (brilliantly paid homage to by Murderface on *Metalocalypse*), caged vixens in geometric war paint, Klaus's damnably persistent retreating hairline. Good times. Great music.

Nineteen ninety's "Wind of Change" served as a career capper for Scorpions' '80s pop star run, but what a grand slam to go out on. Removed from context, this musing on the end of the Cold War—people whose lives had literally been split apart by the just-collapsed Berlin Wall—might sound like any power ballad, but palpable emotion pours forth from the opening whistles onward.

"Wind of Change" functioned as the bridge connecting the newly opened second world to the possibilities of the first—chief among them the freedom to rock. It recast the Scorpions as unofficial ambassadors, who even got to publicly powwow with Soviet perestroika mastermind Mikhail Gorbachev.

Scorpions and Metallica toured together as part of the legendary, Van Halen-headlined Monsters of Rock lineup in 1988. But what the bands share more than that is a genius for vocalizing truths they experience along with their audience. Whether it's Scorpions crystallizing unequal parts hope and fear in "Wind of Change" or Metallica perfectly capturing rage and rapture among "dirtbags" and other factions of the disenfranchised, the bond between performer and fan is unbreakable because it comes off as so unmistakably authentic.

Allow me a personal detour regarding Scorpions here. I spent the '80s as a spike-headed, safety-pinned punk rocker. Metallica opened me up to heavy metal because their music hit me the same way my favorite punk had. If these guys could be the real deal, I reasoned, then there must be more to the long-haired denim-and-leather pool from which they have sprung. And, of course, there was.

This relates to Scorpions for me thusly: I also spent the '80s unhealthily amusing myself (the hard way) in and around New York City's Times Square, which was then the sleaze capital of all unholy creation. Forty-Second Street—aka "the Deuce"—served as the area's vital jizz- and junk-clogged artery. Peep shows, grind-house movies, porn theaters, live sex, streetwalkers, pimps, hustlers, freaks, weirdoes, outcasts, runaways, reprobates, berserk fire-and-brimstone preachers—the Deuce was the greatest open-air brown-ring circus our species has known since the glorious reign of Caligula.

Yet I could find no punk song that ever got it right. Not even close. And I still can't.

"I Slept in an Arcade" by Black Randy and the Metro Squad nails the Hollywood Boulevard equivalent. "Saturday Night at the Bookstore" by the Dicks does the same for Austin, Texas. But the closest New York punk comes (pun, as always, intended) is the Ramones' "53rd & 3rd," bassist Dee Dee's serrated-edge recollection of turning tricks for dope a few blocks northeast of Times Square (and a song covered enthusiastically by Metallica on Rob Zombie's Ramones tribute *We're a Happy Family*).

Still, that was not my experience of the Deuce. To finally hear what I felt on Forty-Second Street in musical form, it took Germans.

"The Zoo" by Scorpions from, appropriately, *Animal Magnetism*, recounts the band's Deuce adventure—even purring "For-tee Seh-CUNT Street" by name—during their 1979 world tour stop in New York.

The music, as described by Martin Popoff in *Top 500 Heavy Metal Songs of All Time*, is at once "ominously slow and melodically accessible," and made buoyant by Klaus's "Berlin burlesque vocal."

The thrill, the menace, the promise, the decadence, the neon, the filth, the heat, the horror—it's all there in five minutes and twenty-eight seconds.

That it's called "The Zoo" is the fisted bung-cherry atop this delectably unsanitary confection.

Best of all, the Deuce is decades gone now, but "The Zoo" will always be there for us. Just drop the needle and go back. Then do it again. And again.

SWEET SAVAGE

Sweet Savage served as the premier showcase of Northern Ireland guitar shaman Vivian Campbell and holds the distinction of not only being covered by Metallica, but actually driving the band to fisticuffs.

One legendary early Metallica gig included an encore of "Let It Loose" by Savage, but Lars Ulrich opted, instead, the pound out the intro to "Killing Time" by Sweet Savage—precisely because it immediately launches into a psychotic drum attack.

James Hetfield, thrown off and helpless to properly recall the lyrics, rewarded Lars's deviation from the set list by slugging the drummer in the stomach. Onstage.

Hetfield, like the other members, was certainly familiar with the Sweet Savage rocker. He just wasn't ready. "Killing Time," in fact, was one of the songs Metallica performed at their very first shows, hoping that the crowd wouldn't know it was somebody else's composition.

In addition, "Killing Time" also appeared on Metallica's very first demo tape in 1982, as well as on the B side of the 1991 monster hit "The Unforgiven."

It's interesting, then, that "Killing Time" was a Sweet Savage B side, as well, paired with "Take No Prisoners"—a one-two hammer blow of dizzying twin-guitar acrobatics and charging metal firestorms. That single alone made Sweet Savage a key element of the New Wave of British Heavy Metal.

And then—that was it.

Vivian Campbell departed Sweet Savage in 1982 to play for Dio. Cofounder and co-axe-master Trevor Fleming called it quits for a spell, then reformed the band without Viv in 1984, for an incarnation that dribbled through the rest of the decade while never releasing a full-length album.

Campbell, in the meantime, bounced from Dio to Whitesnake to Def Leppard to, most recently, a slot with the band who initially inspired them all: Thin Lizzy.

Metallica featured "Killing Time" on the 1998 *Garage Inc.* covers albums, which also includes their popular version of Thin Lizzy's "Whiskey in the Jar."And if you think that's a coincidence, what have you been drinking?

TYGERS OF PAN TANG

Whitley Bay, UK, natives Tygers of Pan Tang mined metal's most worshipped sci-fi author, Michael Moorcock, for their moniker. Specifically, they named themselves after the ferocious animals in Moorcock's *Elric of Melniboné* book series.

These cosmic beasts set out, straightaway, to blow minds. Among those most profoundly detonated was that belonging to teenage Lars Ulrich who, in late winter 1981, placed an ad in the L.A. classified sheet *The Recycler* stating:

"Drummer looking for other metal musicians to play with. Tygers of Pan Tang, Diamond Head, and Iron Maiden."

Those two sentences directly brought about the meeting of Ulrich and James Hetfield. It's significant to note, then, which band Lars listed first.

In September 1979, Neat Records issued the Tygers single "Don't Touch Me There" (making them labelmates with fellow Metallica favorites Blitzkrieg, Raven, and Venom).

Gigs opening for Budgie and Scorpions ensued. The Tygers' instant camaraderie (plus no small dose of competitiveness) with contemporaries such as Saxon, Sweet Savage, and Tank—to say nothing of fellow felines Def Leppard and Jaguar—further established them as fighting figureheads among the New Wave of British Heavy Metal.

After releasing *The Cage* on MCA in 1982, the record company insisted Tygers record more cover tunes. Bizarrely, the song being most forcefully thrust upon them was the '60s chestnut "Love Potion No. 9."

Unable to break free from MCA (or, in good conscience, to get themselves to do "Love Potion No. 9"), Tygers disbanded, reforming in 1985 and issuing *The Wreck-Age* on indie label Music for Nations, the very outfit that brilliantly handled the UK releases of Metallica's first three albums.

Alas, in two years' time (subsequent post-1999 reunion shows and releases notwithstanding) Tygers of Pan Tang became, in essence, an extinct species.

What lives on, of course, is their role in the creation of Metallica and, more importantly, their music—wild, saber-toothed, and ever positioned to pounce.

VENOM

To find the original wellspring of "metal played with punk attitude," explorers need not look much further than Newcastle's glorious slop squad Venom.

From their first perfectly bungled breakdown, these Satan-serenading ghouligans took on the tag "punks with long hair."

The music of Venom is speedy, thrashing, and fixated on death. It forced metal to previous unrealized extremes. This makes Venom, thereby, the forefathers of speed, thrash, death, and, in fact, all extreme metal. And then, as if they needed another founding credit, Venom released an iconic album in 1982 titled *Black Metal*.

It's no wonder that nearly every early photograph of Metallica depicts at least one member in a Venom T-shirt.

In 1984, Metallica rushed to take Venom on tour. Two decades later, they offered no return (hell)fire a when singer Cronos (nee Conrad Lant) suggested that Metallica—who had gone, in his mind, to "crap"—remove the word *metal* from their name.

That's respect—possibly on both parties' parts.

BLACKENED: BLACK METAL

The sound is grinding, desperate, and, for sure, evil. Often the recording is shoddy and tinny and it hurts to hear, making the music all that much more sinister and effective.

Born of Venom (specifically in the song "Black Metal"), nurtured by Bathory and Hellhammer, and then unleashed, lethally, throughout Lars Ulrich's original northern European stomping grounds, black metal is the sound of Satan's sons advancing up out of the flames of their personal hells to infect the planet with demonic unrest.

In the early 1990s' wake of Metallica's (coincidentally nicknamed) Black Album, black metal proper's major contribution to culture arrived via Norwegian nutcases who, splashed in black-and-white "corpse paint," set out to prove they were no posers in the most maniacal manners imaginable, via murder, suicide, mutilation, suicide, and torching a succession of thousand-year-old churches.

You're only supposed to sing about that stuff, dudes! Better still, do what Dave Mustaine did when he got the boot from Metallica: He started Megadeth!

Black Metal Basics

Bathory: *Bathory, Return of the Darkness and Evil,*
   Under the Sign of the Black Mark, Blood Fire Death
Carpathian Forest—*Morbid Fascination of Death*
Cradle of Filth—*Dusk and Her Embrace, Crüelty and the Beast*
Darkthrone—*A Blaze in the Northern Sky*
Destruction—*Sentence of Death*
Emperor—*In the Nightside Eclipse*
Enslaved—*Frost, Eld, Mardraum, Isa*
Hellhammer—*Apocalyptic Raids*

Marduk—*Plague Angel*
Mayhem—*Pure Fucking Armageddon*
Sigh—*Imaginary Soniscape, Hangman's Hymn, Scenes from Hell*
Venom—*Welcome to Hell, Black Metal, At War with Satan*

From Queens, New York, the Ramones. (Photofest)

4

SEEK AND DESTROY:
PUNK, HARDCORE, AND INDUSTRIAL

The official approved New York-L.A. rock critic rap on punk rock is that, by the mid-1970s, capital-*R* Rock was getting boring and bloated (the names such bozos always invoke as examples are prog gods Yes and Emerson, Lake and Palmer) and then, lucky for humanity, narcotized ectomorphs and art school androgynoids from Manhattan saved the world and hooray—we're us!

Do you think that story and those zeros could actually be the origin of the music that powers Metallica?

Now, the facts: Punk started when four metal fans in black jeans, the Ramones, couldn't pull off the technical dexterity to play metal properly, so they invented a savage, frantic take on it, directly addressing what was most important to them: girls, monster movies, late-night TV, sniffing glue, Nazi jokes, and hating yourself.

Punk was perfected the following year when guttersnipe metalhead Johnny Rotten auditioned for a peculiar spin on the boy-band gimmick by singing Alice Cooper's "I'm Eighteen." Thusly, the Sex Pistols scored their mangled mouthpiece.

The filth and the fury of punk tapped directly into the main line of teenage angst and blew out the back end with omnidirectional abandon. Instead of metal's sorcery and Satanism, though, punk songs addressed real, desperate times in a really desperate fashion.

In time, punk evolved into subgenres such as hardcore, indus-

trial, and, yes, thrash. What they shared in common was screaming immediacy and tribal passion.

Metallica plugged right into those same feelings and rode the
Mohawk-headed lightning.

ANTI-NOWHERE LEAGUE

"So fucking whuuut?" gobs Animal, front man for über-punk
knuckle-bucklers the Anti-Nowhere League as the opening to
1981's "So What," the band's paradoxically ripping ode to apathy.

Metallica covers "So What?" as the B side of the 1991 "Sad
but True" single, with James Hetfield going full cockney while the
band bashes it out in proper pogo-invoking homage to the original.

It's a blast. How could it not be?

The music is crazy shambling hostility driving words that
invoke intimate relations with the Queen, Bach, an old man, a
sheep, and a goat, punctuated by drugs and self-abuse.

Yeah. So what?

Long a live favorite, Animal joined Metallica onstage at Wembley Stadium on October 25, 1992, for a boot-stomping tear-up
of "So What."

Remembering it on the Anti-Nowhere League website, Animal
wrote: "As I waited on the edge of the stage waiting to go on,
it suddenly dawned on me I was just about to stand in front of
10,000 punters who didn't know me from Adam and sing a song
that I couldn't fucking remember; all that kept running through
my head was RUN you silly old fucker!"

As popular YouTube footage of the performance attests, Animal matched Metallica's energy and showed off what had inspired
them to pay tribute to the Anti-Nowhere League in the first place.

And if he had run?

Well . . . SO WHAT!

BLACK FLAG

In punk circles, Black Flag's four-bar logo is as ubiquitous as upside-
down crosses in the metal universe. Each conveys the same cosmic

import, stating: "Looking for the back door into an underworld of limitless expression? Look no further."

As did Metallica, Black Flag continually expanded the boundaries of their defined genre to the point that such boundaries no longer existed: metal or punk—rock was rock, you just had to be awesome at it.

In fact, what the Southern California bruisers in Black Flag did for punk remarkably parallels Metallica's transformation of heavy metal.

Specifically, both bands cross-pollinated music forms, defied gospel traditions, and blazed the very touring trails that hard rock up-and-comers continue to traverse today.

At the height of their popularity, Black Flag even scandalized their fuzz-skulled brethren by growing their hair long. And we all know what happened to Metallica's flowing coifs once they decided to take on the biggest challengers on the planet.

Much is made of the mid-'80s punk-metal "crossover," most often by invoking Metallica and other thrash acts. Hardcore heavy hitters like D.R.I. and Cro-Mags also come up, but it seems as though Black Flag—properly praised elsewhere—gets short shrift for their crucial role in this revolutionary musical miscegenation.

It's goofy to think about it now, but in 1985, living fistfight front man Henry Rollins's hippie-length locks really did shock the safety pins out Black Flag's constituents, particularly given the group's pure-punk history.

With a tyrannical work ethic, founding guitarist Greg Ginn shepherded the group from its earliest incarnation to full fruition in the '70s-turning-'80s L.A. moment that also whelped the Germs, X, Fear, and the Circle Jerks (whose Keith Morris started in Black Flag).

Three singers in, in 1981, Rollins took the mic, and Black Flag rapidly evolved into an unprecedented touchstone for furious young outcasts, with the violence of the music erupting frequently at their shows onstage, off-stage, backstage, and everywhere else.

Musically, Black Flag's similarities to Metallica are subtle but self-evident (louder, harder, deeper). But when James Hetfield talks about how directly punk lyrics spoke to him, consider how Rollins's words dovetail with Hetfield's lyrical viewpoints—be they social, personal, or even knuckleheaded.

The aforementioned spirit of iconoclasm further unites the groups. While playing in Black Flag, Ginn ran SST Records, one of the premier groundbreaking hard rock indie labels of the '80s, whose artist lineup was brazenly eclectic.

Beyond fellow punks like Hüsker Dü and the Minutemen, the SST roster showcased doom metal pioneers Saint Vitus, the guitar-solo-obsessed Dinosaur Jr., and future grunge stars Soundgarden and Screaming Trees.

Black Flag truly drew a line in the mosh pit, however, with the release of *My War* in 1984. While other hardcore bands solidified their sound into a formula of ever faster and shorter outbursts, *My War*'s songs are slow and dense and complex. In short: They're metal.

The subsequent incarnation of Black Flag incorporated blues, free jazz, and extended instrumental passages, propelling the perimeters of their sound so far afield that they ultimately came apart in 1986—just as thrash took over.

In the wake of Black Flag's demise, Henry Rollins has remained the group's most high-profile member, an outspoken jack-of-all-trades whose books detailing the band's touring life lay out, again, similarities to Metallica in both spirit and specifics.

When talking about influences, Rollins routinely cites Van Halen, Ted Nugent, and Black Oak Arkansas—names that were sacrilege to the Mohawk-adorned faithful of the day.

And akin to Cliff Burton turning Metallica on to the Misfits by constantly playing Danzig and company's tapes in the bus, Rollins recounts the Black Flag van rocking repeatedly to Deep Purple, ZZ Top's *Eliminator*, and *Mob Rules* by Black Sabbath. Bear in mind that, back then, even the most diehard metalheads were loath to invoke Dio-era Sab over Ozzy.

Further invoking R.E.M.-lover Cliff Burton, Greg Ginn engaged in the ultimate hard rock heresy via the book *Our Band Could Be Your Life* by Michael Azerrad.

When asked to name the group he adores more than any other, Ginn says: "The Grateful Dead—if there's one favorite band I have, that's probably that. I saw them maybe seventy-five times."

Balls that big are both punk and metal, indeed.

BUTTHOLE SURFERS

At a 1983 gig by art-rock terrorists the Right to Eat Fred Astaire's Asshole, fifteen-year-old drummer King Coffey could barely believe what the underwear-clad singer was spewing forth.

"They were playing Bloodrock's 'D.O.A.,'" Koffey recalls, "the most uncool song in the world for a hardcore punk rock band to be playing."

That, of course, made it the epitome of cool. It also marked the birth of Texas psych-freaks the Butthole Surfers, after Koffey combined forces with Astaire's Asshole vocalist Gibby Haynes, guitarist Paul Leary, and, later, co-percussionist Teresa Nervosa.

For lack of any clue of where else to put them, Butthole Surfers records get filed under "punk" but, as evidenced by that initial epiphany, metal has always surged through the muck-pumping heart of this dangerous coven's sideshow soul.

Because, really: "D.O.A." by Bloodrock!?!

A fluke #36 hit in 1971, it's an unbearably heavy eight-and-half-minute prog slog—complete with organ solos and siren sounds—sung from the point of view of a non-survivor of an airplane crash.

However stunning it was for Metallica to cover the Misfits at a time when metal and punk remained violently divided, this was even more outrageous, because, as with Metallica, the band's affection for the original was heartfelt and sincere.

In 1987, the same year that Metallica declared their punk ties official on *Garage Days Re-Revisited*, the Butthole Surfers opened their magnum opus *Locust Abortion Technician* with "Sweat Loaf." It's not so much a cover of Black Sabbath's "Sweet Leaf" as it is a psychic demolition and cosmic reconstruction of the song.

"Sweat Loaf," along with the rest of *Locust Abortion Technician* and its 1988 follow-up, *Hairway to Steven*, is the sound of inspired stoners so in love with Black Sabbath and Led Zeppelin (et al) that they dive into the music itself and bend it and stretch it and mold it and wrap themselves in it and then blow the whole thing up so that they can do it all over again. (The Buttholes' major-label hit, 1994's *Independent Worm Saloon*, was even produced by Zep's John Paul Jones.)

The Butthole Surfers magically reinvented punk with the very sounds that punk sought to sink into the tar pits of history: Here now, from Texas, arose dinosaur rock reborn as an entire flock of acid-dripping dragons.

Metallica did the same for metal, re-creating it as accessible and identifiable to kids with pins in their nostrils, wardrobes full of flannel, and Buttholes on their brains.

DIE KRUPPS

Metallica stunned many by covering death-dance pillagers Killing Joke on *Garage Days Re-Revisited*, so perhaps it shouldn't have come as such a surprise in 1992 when German industrialists Die Krupps returned the nod with their own covers collection—consisting of nothing but Metallica songs and titled, fittingly, *A Tribute to Metallica*.

Die Krupps would later oversee the multi-artist project *The Blackest Album: An Industrial Tribute to Metallica*, a four-volume series of albums where headbanging anthems get the pulse-pounding electro run-through.

There is more to this Teutonic thud-factory, of course, than attempting to make Kirk Hammett's leads sound a little bit disco-ish.

Pulsating to nasty life in 1982, Die Krupps initially sounded much like industrial bedrocks Throbbing Gristle and Cabaret Voltaire—electronic cacophony powered by punishing beats.

After a long ten years of stagnation, the band reemerged with down-tuned guitars pushed way up front, effectively pulling the plug on industrial as a punk offshoot and jacking it into pure, evil metal, and essentially configuring what the genre would sound like, and slay like, for the next two decades.

All it took was an unhealthy dose of Metallica.

DIRTY ROTTEN IMBECILES (D.R.I.)

Hardcore Houstonites Dirty Rotten Imbeciles—D.R.I. for logo-friendly short—relocated to San Francisco in 1983. It was the perfect time and time and place for punks going metal, as, mere months after Metallica's *Kill 'Em All* debut, the local metal scene tumbled inexorably toward punk.

Prior to this, and for some years onward, the divide was clear and often defined by violence: Punk and metal existed as enemy sounds, philosophies and lifestyles, with each camp's adherents ever ready to take up arms against the other.

That was so stupid, wasn't it?

Let us give thanks, then, for these Imbeciles, among others (not the least of whom was Cliff Burton and his Misfits obsession), who put an end to such   well, actual imbecility.

Socially outspoken and indisputably hardcore in attitude (even traveling with the Dead Kennedys on the "Rock Against Reagan" tour), D.R.I. nonetheless consistently inched in a metal direction musically until they finally made the melding of the forms official in 1987 by unleashing an album titled, in no uncertain terms, *Cross-over*.

While contemporaries such as Suicidal Tendencies, Corrosion of Conformity, Cro-Mags, and others were also actively picking up on what Motörhead, Discharge, and the Exploited had started (and what Metallica perfected), D.R.I. gave the movement, and its moment, a perfect handle.

That the *Crossover* record was great and that, live, the band blew crowds away every time backed this bridging of the gap with iron-clad credibility.

No longer did skinheads have to be on guard at metal shows, and no longer did headbangers have to prepare to punch their way out of hardcore venues. Hard rock, done right, united everyone.

Metallica played it. D.R.I named it. The world has rocked harder ever since.

DISCHARGE

They're often associated with the genre "crust punk," and the term "discharge" might conjure images of an oozing scab, but for the band Discharge, think more in terms of "discharging a firearm."

Like the one on the front of a tank. Then add an infantry behind them. And, then, in unison . . . fire!

Discharge came about in 1977 and, fronted by Kevin "Cal" Morris from 1981 onward, the band executed a grave-black aural acid assault so constructively virulent that it spawned its own subgenre—the grinding, distorted, brutally political D-beat (also known as "Discrust")—and directly inspired (at least) the next two generations of metal.

"Free Speech for the Dumb" is the Discharge cover on *Garage Inc.* As in the original, the lyrics consist entirely of the title being repeated over and over again. Violently. The guitar, the drums, the hatred—they're all colossal. And crushing.

In a 2008 *Rolling Stone* issue dedicated to rock's top vocalists, Hetfield named Cal Morris as one of the greatest singers of all time.

He would know.

THE EXPLOITED

"Punk's not dead!" proclaimed Scottish true believers the Exploited in 1981. That was also the title of their first album, and the idea that rushed through the record's fifteen chain-saw blurts of pogo vexation as well as the band's steel-toes-to-your-suddenly-gushing-nose live shows.

Troops of Tomorrow, Exploited's 1982 follow-up, ratcheted up the rants and chants to perfect-specimen status: For an example of political punk in transition from the first wave of the Clash and the Sex Pistols toward hardcore, crust, and industrial to come, just slap on this platter.

There is something very dumb about the Exploited, and that's not necessarily a knock. If you replaced "Christ" with "Maggie" (as in Thatcher) and "evil" with "anarchy," the Exploited's anti-establishment rage matched that of metal's most muddle-skulled amateur sorcerers.

The Exploited were the first high-profile punks to really, seriously dress at all times as though they were wearing Halloween "punk rocker" costumes (neon-hued Mohawks, million-studded motorcycle jackets, plaid trousers, and all that). On top of that,

Troops contains a song titled "Sid Vicious Was Innocent" (wasn't "innocence" the opposite of his—and by extension their—entire shtick?).

Such blunt brainlessness, though, can provide an ideal, unvarnished vehicle for visceral, gut-punch honesty. There, Exploited delivered in brilliantly stupid spades.

They grew toward metal with each successive album (although I wouldn't want to have told them that at the time within switchblade-slashing distance), and for the American metal bands moshing toward a punk crossover, Exploited provided wonder nitro for the fuel tanks of thrash.

In early-'80s San Francisco, members of Exodus and Testament were particularly outspoken fans. Young James Hetfield routinely played Metallica shows in an Exploited T-shirt.

At the same time in New York, *Troops of Tomorrow*'s calls for united fronts and resistance to the Man pushed mooks who otherwise would have just gone metal into inventing themselves as CBGB hardcore matinee staples such as Agnostic Front and Cro-Mags.

In 1993, Slayer teamed with Ice-T (still in his speed-metal Body Count mode) to cover Exploited's "Disorder" for the *Judgment Night* soundtrack.

And that Mohawk-adorned skeleton all over stickers and shirts at your local mall's rock store? That comes from the Exploited too.

Their punk really isn't dead.

G.B.H.

British punks who went to war with dancey British "post-punk" by going even punker—which is to say, more metallic—G.B.H. stormed the gutters gunning under the moniker "Charged G.B.H.," a reference to singer Colin Abrahall's arrest for "Grievous Bodily Harm" (there was also another band named G.B.H. at the time, but these spitfires made short order of them, right quick enough).

Leather, Bristles, No Survivors and Sick Boys, the band's 1981 singles compilation, is a forerunner of black metal in terms of its title, scrappy assemblage, and roughshod production values.

G.B.H.'s debut album pulls off the same trick even more dramatically with thrash and death metal, by being called *City Baby Attacked by Rats* and boasting a sound that, frankly, thrashes.

Pick a random photo of teenage Metallica and odds are high that one of them is bedecked in a G.B.H. shirt. Listening to G.B.H. will make you immediately understand that couture choice—as well as why Slayer would go on to cover this punk outfit the way Metallica covered the Misfits.

KILLING JOKE

On *Garage Days Re-Revisited*, Metallica maps out a path that connects Budgie to Blitzkrieg to the Misfits. It's a Big Picture moment at which, potentially, others may well have arrived.

The EP's real left turn comes in "The Wait," originally by UK post-punk proselytizers Killing Joke.

Killing Joke?

"Green Hell/Last Caress" was startling enough, so "The Wait" was a real baffler: What did this death-disco art school grooviness have to do with the doom-mongering of the old gods, the amphetamine leather-crack of the New Wave of British Heavy Metal, or the hammer-pogo bloodletting of hardcore punk?

Metallica answers that question immediately in "The Wait," from the hot-scalpel slices of the opening riffs to the tribal percussion throughout to the cascading chorus that swoops upward like an anthem for the apocalypse.

To hear "The Wait" is to comprehend, "Ah! This, too, is metal"—and to feel where industrial music came from and where it went in the next decade.

Sometimes even the most extreme music really does have a good beat and you can dance to it. With a girl, even.

THE MISFITS

From hell they came—okay, it was actually Lodi, New Jersey—and with the first needle-drop on their first 1977 seven-inch (the eerily guitar-free "Cough Cool"/"She"), the Misfits rocketed from the tombs of '50s hip-swivel switchblade cool, up through a bombastic black-and-white onslaught of monster movies, comic books, busted fuzz-boxes, UFO abductions, Halloween pranks gone apocalyptic, and endless loops of the Zapruder film.

Immediately and irrevocably, this band splattered itself all over antiestablishment culture in every form it would take for the next four decades.

Like an incarnation of the Ramones that could only play it serial-killer straight, the Misfits launched three-chord, rippingly melodic rock 'n' roll anthems at breakneck velocity in bone-snap-size blasts.

They also looked like the music sounds: a quartet of berserk, leather-clad musclemen in zombie makeup with grease-twisted ropes of hair geometrically bisecting their faces.

Fronting this fright force was singer-songwriter Glenn Danzig, an Elvis-Jim Morrison obsessive. Cofounder Jerry Only played bass. Several guitarists cycled through the band before Jerry's brother Doyle proved the perfect fret-wrecker. Same with drummers: Arthur Googy provided great early beats before legendary punk producer Robo manned the kit.

As an unholy musical meeting ground between Alice Cooper, the Ramones, Black Sabbath, Kiss, Venom, and Black Flag—while remaining in an outrageous league of their own—the Misfits prototypically demonstrated, and perhaps even made inevitable, the later-'80s punk-metal crossover.

No band more fully embodied that crossover than Metallica. And what band did they use to make the declaration of the moment official? The Misfits. Of course.

Lars Ulrich recalls Cliff Burton commandeering the tour bus tape deck and "just pounding out this Misfits stuff." Kirk Hammett adds: "It just kind of grew on us. I liked the songs and then I saw the pictures of them and went, 'Wow! This is cool!'"

Millions of previously punk-shunning heavy metal fans enjoyed the same reaction with the arrival Metallica's game-changing 1987 covers romp, *The $5.98 EP: Garage Days Re-Revisited*.

What was hinted at by Cliff Burton wearing a partially obscured Misfits skull logo shirt on the back cover of *Master of Puppets*—and more clearly by Misfits covers performed live—came to history-making vinyl fruition via *Garage Days'* closing medley of the Misfits' "Last Caress" and "Green Hell."

From then on, metal and punk not only made peace, they made beautifully anti-beautiful music together.

Metallica went on to champion Glenn Danzig's post-Misfits projects: the unsung and enormously influential Samhain, along with his eponymous super-heavy spook squad Danzig. At numerous gigs where Danzig opened for Metallica in 1994, he joined them onstage to belt out Misfits covers.

The Misfits and Metallica have benefited more from each one another's existence more than any other two bands in hard rock —perhaps even in all of rock, period.

And all along, all either one of them wanted—and needed— were your skulls.

NICK CAVE

Of all the curious covers Metallica performs, none proves more brain-boggling to headbangers than "Loverman" on *Garage Inc.* The original is by sharp-dressed Australian ghoul Nick Cave and his backing ectomorphs the Bad Seeds.

Despite lyrical references to sex and disease and bound hands and a devil who waits and crawls and lies by your side, anything by Nick Cave might seem an ill fit for Metallica. But there it is. And for many, "Loverman" works.

There have been critics, though, and it was they who James Hetfield addressed after the controversial mid-'90s reception of *Load* and *ReLoad*. Surprising many, he came out hard as a fan of dark, soulful songwriters Tom Waits, Leonard Cohen, and, yes, Nick Cave.

What Nick Cave does share with Metallica is an infatuation with the savagery and lawlessness, as well as the promise of redemption and new beginnings, of America's Old West and Deep South— or at least that version of it in pulp fiction, frontier ballads, and cowboy movies, in particular spaghetti westerns.

Hetfield has spoken often of his fanatical worship of *The Good, the Bad, and the Ugly* (1966) as well as of an ongoing interest in country music.

Cave's devotion goes further. Musically, he collaborated with Johnny Cash, even dueting with him on a Hank Williams song. In 1989, Cave wrote an acclaimed Southern Gothic novel, *And the Ass Saw the Angel*. Fifteen years later, he composed the screenplay for *The Proposition* (2005), a blisteringly violent western set during the 1880s in Australia's outback.

The outlaw gene ropes Metallica and Nick Cave together. Their message is the same, too: Saddle up and forget about the marked trail—just ride hard and aim to die with your boots on. Or in Nick's case, your fancy Italian loafers. Okay, in Lars's case, too.

THE RAMONES

"Like Sabbath, the Ramones were a quantum leap in sound and design," writes Joe Carducci in *Rock and the Pop Narcotic*.

Metallica mounted the same paradigm rupture a mere half-decade after the Ramones' 1976 debut, because, yet again, it was time. Somebody had to shake shit up.

As Thomas Jefferson once put it: "The tree of liberty must be refreshed from time to time, with the blood of patriots and tyrants. It is its natural manure." The same is true of rock 'n' roll, just re-place "patriots and tyrants" with "metalheads and punks." But leave in the manure part. That's cool.

Four ugly weirdheads who took their band name from Paul McCartney's hotel check-in alias, the Ramones hailed from scenic Queens, New York. In the '70s, NYC's outer boroughs were as remote from the glamour and hoi polloi nonsense of Manhattan as Iowa or Helsinki or Timbuktu, despite being a mere fifty-cent subway token and a half-hour away (see *All in the Family* or *Saturday Night Fever* for a glimpse of how it really was, especially if you're reading this now in the vicinity of—bleccch—contemporary Brooklyn).

The Ramones never intended to create punk rock, particularly that first strain of it that became so quickly polluted with high-art swine and fashionista gargoyles. Like Metallica, these greasy outcasts were rock fans who wanted to be rock stars. Their aim was to compete in stadiums against Aerosmith and Ted Nugent. That they only made it to CBGB alongside Patti Smith and the Voidoids seems, all at once, tragically unfair, unfortunate, and inevitable.

Okay, the Ramones did eventually get big enough to endlessly play medium-size theaters, and they did get to star in *Rock 'n' Roll High School*, one of the greatest movies ever, and they did get to tour with Sabbath in '78, one of the greatest mismatches ever, in terms of what audiences could handle at the time. But the grand prize—the sort of galaxy-conquering master move Metallica pulled off with the Black Album—forever eluded them. But not the rest of the world.

Ten years after the final Ramones show in 1996, the sound they created thoroughly dominated and defined mainstream rock music. Green Day, who went on to rival Metallica among the biggest of all hard rock acts, did so by sticking close to the Ramones' sound while also coming off, to young fans, as "cute."

Cute, the Ramones could not do.

Metallica has spoken often about how punk lyrics moved them more directly than a lot of metal bands' sword-and-surgery expositions. The very first Ramones song ever is called "I Don't Care," with its titular phrase comprising twelve of the song's eighteen total words, minimally conveying a vast universe of hurt.

So why didn't the Ramones crack the biggest of the big time? There is the physical grotesquerie of the performers, but then that hasn't exactly impeded Lemmy. And then there is the simplicity of the music, but that's only propelled AC/DC up to and beyond the stratosphere.

The answer is: sex. Lemmy, warts and all, is a biker-pirate-reichmarschall god-thing whose libidinal juju thunders through his every bass note and dragon-breathed intonation. AC/DC is essentially the sound of sex itself: building, pounding, sliding, building pounding, sliding, exploding, then done.

The music of the Ramones, however powerful, is not entirely sexless; it just hates itself for whatever sex is there. Because unlike at Motörhead or AC/DC arena orgies, once the guy in the pinhead mask left the stage with the "Gabba-Gabba-Hey!" sign, no panties littered the floors of a Ramones performance.

The Ramones' isolation and rage and self-loathing is all directed inward. What comes out can be comedic, but every jape is a
plea, every chuckle exists to postpone a weeping and wailing and
gnashing of teeth just behind the humor. Metallica got it. And they
give it, too, in their own style.

Consider the six Ramones songs Metallica has covered.

"Commando"—A maybe ironic, maybe not jingoistic pump-
up for grunts getting ready to blast Vietnam. Guitarist Johnny
Ramone remained, until his demise in 2004 from cancer, one of
rock's most outspoken right-wingers. Sans any outward political
pronouncements, there is nearly as much Johnny Ramone in James
Hetfield as there is Ted Nugent. And that's a whole lot of dead
commies' worth.

"Today Your Love/Tomorrow the World"—Metal, by its nature, is right-wing: It's traditional(ist), hyper-focused, and elitist
in that it's difficult to play. Punk is left-wing: It spurns tradition,
blurs established boundaries, and is egalitarian in that the whole
idea is that anyone can play it. A pop-infused hard rock love song
paraphrasing Adolf Hitler and including words that include a
"Nazi-shotzi" pledge to fight for the fatherland, as this one does,
straddles the line perfectly. After all, how far is it from a pogo-
dance to a goose step? And how perverse to make it such a giddy
sing-along?

"Now I Wanna Sniff Some Glue"—Getting high however you
can when you're too young to get high on anything other than
what you can easily get your mitts on— whether it's from huffing
model airplane fumes or obsessing over NWOBHM rarities—is yet
another shared experience of the Ramones-Metallica nexus.

"Cretin Hop" Too soon after it broke, punk got tagged
"smart" music, while heavy metal stood perpetually shunned as
stupid noise for noisy stupids. The Ramones countered here, by
singing, "D-U-M-B! / Everyone's accusing me!" Metallica joyfully
echoes that defiance.

"We're a Happy Family"—Adopted as a unifying anthem for
punks, this speedy flamethrower hints at the sick, scary homes that
produce misfits who stray into hard rock. Nobody in the Ramones

grew up in circumstances conducive to them becoming anything other than Ramones. Metallica knew where they were coming from.

"53rd & 3rd"—True tales from junkie bassist Dee Dee Ramone's teenage career as a street prostitute selling gay sex for dope money. This is as dark and deep as the Ramones got, because it was as open and honest as any band as ever been—including Metallica. The protagonist, an egomaniac with an inferiority complex, bemoans both the fact that he's hustling and the fact that he gets passed over for other hustlers. Until he can stand it no more. "Then I took out my razor blade and I did what God forbade / Now the cops are after me but I proved that I'm no sissy." There's a smile in Lars Hetfield's voice as he chimes in on that part, but it's not one of joy. It's from recognizing the relief of a real confession.

The truth hurts, but it also makes you free. Three chords at a time.

DAMAGE INC.
Industrial Rock

Static, feedback, drones, tape loops, synthesizers, sequencers, drum programs, and general amplified electronic mayhem played with punk attitude and, for the past twenty years, metal guitars that you can (sometimes) dance to: That is industrial music.

As far afield as that might seem, Metallica has proven to be both an inspiration and a point of emulation for industrial rock. Germany's Die Krupps has covered Metallica repeatedly and overseen a series of industrial tribute albums to them.

What began as punishingly inaccessible avant-garde rackets from England's Throbbing Gristle and Germany's Einstürzende Neubauten went a bit New Wave in the '80s with Front 242, Nitzer Ebb, and Skinny Puppy before bulldozing clearly into metal terrain with Ministry, Nine Inch Nails, and Rammstein.

Bearing Metallica in mind, submit to the following steel-punching jackhammer slam-downs to see how extreme music truly is a big, welcoming barbwire-enclosed camp.

Bloodyminded—*Magnetism*

Cabaret Voltaire—*Red Mecca*

Die Krupps—*Metalmorphosis, Tribute to Metallica*

Front 242—*Front by Front*

Einstürzende Neubauten—*Kollaps, Drawings of Patient O.T.*

Lou Reed—*Metal Machine Music*

Ministry—*The Land of Rape and Honey, The Mind Is a Terrible Thing to Taste, Psalm 69*

Nine Inch Nails—*Pretty Hate Machine, The Downward Spiral*

Rammstein—*Sehnsucht, Mutter, Liebe Ist Für Alle Da*

Skinny Puppy—*VIVIsectVI, Too Dark Park My Apocalypse*

Throbbing Gristle—*20 Jazz Funk Greats*

Whitehouse—*Great White Death*

Wolf Eyes—*Burned Mind, Black Vomit*

NEW YORK PUNK

Once the self-titled Ramones debut landed in 1976, punk was among us. Bowery bar CBGB hosted the nascent scene, which spread to London rapidly, and Los Angeles right after that.

New York punk started out arty and eclectic—Blondie, Talking Heads, and Patti Smith–but it eventually clotted into hardcore, a violence-driven tribal beatdown soundtrack for mooks who, in most circumstances, would have been metalheads, but they liked to shave their scalps (and then stick broken bottles into each other's).

Metallica picked up much from each moment of the movement.

The Dead Boys—*Young, Loud, and Snotty*

The Dictators—*Go Girl Crazy!*

Johnny Thunders and the Heartbreakers—*L.A.M.F.*

New York Dolls—*New York Dolls, Too Much Too Soon*

The Plasmatics—*New Hope for the Wretched*

The Ramones—*Ramones, Leave Home, Rocket to Russia, Road to Ruin, Too Tough to Die*

Richard Hell and the Voidoids—*Blank Generation*

Suicide—*Suicide*

Television—*Marquee Moon*

Tuff Darts—*Tuff Darts!*

THE THING THAT SHOULD NOT BE
Cliff Burton's Love of R.E.M. and U2

There's a band called R.E.M. that I like a lot," said Cliff Burton in 1985, "strangely enough."

Metallica's original bassist made known his eclectic taste both implicitly, by way of his exquisitely nuanced playing, and explicitly, by simply stating the wide array of artists he admired and from whom he—and by extension Metallica—learned.

First and foremost was composer Johann Sebastian Bach (1685–1750). This is not so surprising, given Burton's classical training and heavy metal's pyrotechnic roots in the baroque style, of which Bach rules as the all-time master.

Secondly, Cliff revered Glenn Danzig. Burton exposed more metalheads to the horror-punk of the Misfits than any other musician, and he forever championed Danzig's follow-up band, the Stooges-influenced spook squad Samhain. Again, the dark themes and diabolical energy don't seem too baffling a leap.

Now we get to R.E.M.

And that is weird.

In every book and every tribute to Burton since his tragic bus accident death in 1986, his love of R.E.M. gets repeatedly mentioned.

"Cliff was responsible for a lot of the musicality of the band," notes rock journalist Martin Popoff in the book *To Live Is to Die*. "His heroes were R.E.M. and Thin Lizzy, specifically for the harmonies—vocal for the former, guitars for the latter."

Given this knowledge, and listening with R.E.M. in mind, the impact on Cliff made by those soft-edged, Southern college-rock icons is palpable. You can hear it when he's unhurried in spots where other bassists might want to just rush forward, and you can hear it in subtle, sophisticated choices he makes that add to each song's overall wallop. It's a feathery touch that works better, when properly employed, as a blending tool than a sledgehammer. For then it sets up the real devastating drop-downs.

Exposed as he was to the Athens, Georgia's finest by Cliff, Lars played tennis against R.E.M. bassist Mike Mills at the 2000 Grand Slam Jam Tennis Shootout, and then they both jammed alongside court legends John McEnroe and Jim Courier in a pickup band.

The other left-field Cliff favorite is U2.

U2 often comes up in the Metallica conversation, but not until talk turns to *Load* and *ReLoad*, the stadium-packing superstar stage.

That is a time James Hetfield does not think back on fondly, insisting that Lars and Kirk Hammett were doing the driving and that they were modeling the direction of the band after U2—who were then the biggest rock attraction on earth, putting on the hugest shows in the history of moving spectacles and who had, with 1991's *Achtung Baby*, gambled on mixing up their general sound and aesthetic.

But what of the U2 that Cliff so loved? In 1986, a full year before they attained their first level of global monstrousness with *The Joshua Tree*, U2 were still college-radio heroes, Irish wastrels who borrowed some energy from punk (they mention the Ramones a lot, but really it's the Clash) and a lot of etherealness from post-punk (in particular, the first Public Image record) to turn alternative rock into just rock, proper.

Perhaps in those early albums, Cliff picked up on U2's ambitions and very particular ability to ride them to unprecedented heights. Lead guitarist the Edge, for better or worse, created a signature style that rewrote the rules of popular music. Metallica was in the same process.

What a tragedy on top of a tragedy that we never got to fully go along where Cliff Burton would have taken these inspirations.

NOTHING ELSE MATTERS
UK Punk

A narchy in the UK" by the Sex Pistols changed rock, which changed culture, which changed the world. Such was the power, in 1977, of that song and that band and the inferno they momentarily crystallized: punk.

When Metallica and the other Bay Area thrash bands talked about loving punk, it was almost always the British version they were espousing (New York's Ramones were the exception).

Here, now, a guide to Her Majesty's Thrashiest Punk Subjects:

The Adverts—*Crossing the Red Sea with the Adverts*

Anti-Nowhere League—*We Are the League*

Buzzcocks—*A Different Kind of Tension*

The Damned—*Damned, Damned, Damned*

Discharge—*Hear Nothing, See Nothing, Say Nothing*

The Exploited—*Punk's Not Dead, Troops of Tomorrow*

G.B.H.—*City Baby Attacked by Rats, City Baby's Revenge*

Sex Pistols—*Never Mind the Bollocks, Here's the Sex Pistols*

Sham 69—*Tell Us the Truth*

Skrewdriver—*All Skrewed Up*

U.K. Subs—*Another Kind of Blues*

Anthrax, circa 1984. (Photofest)

5

WHIPLASH:
THRASH MASTERS UNLIMITED

Power metal, at some point, just wasn't quite powerful enough for a new generation of headbangers.

With nothing but respect for Europe's power metal pioneers (Iron Maiden, Judas Priest, etc.) and their operatic offspring (Helloween, Manowar), in the mid-1980s, the American underground lunged forward into thrash—with Metallica leading the charge.

Metallica, Slayer, Megadeth, and Anthrax would quickly comprise thrash's Big Four, but theirs was a big field of like-minded longhairs who, with outright athletic commitment and effort, forged storm after storm of gigantic, complicated, constantly on-the-go rock.

Thrash upped the punk within the New Wave of British Heavy Metal, injected animal steroids into classic Sabbath doom, and slammed its white leather high-top sneaker all the way down on the gas pedal, all at once.

ACCEPT

Bavarian banshee Udo Dirkschneider separated Germany's Accept from other early-'80s European metal. On record, the lead vocalist's cement-chunk helium shriek made all the difference, while, in videos and onstage, there was no denying the sheer force of Udo's—let us say—"nontraditional" rock star appearance.

Five foot one, clad in camouflage during the age of leather, and built like the world's least adoptable pit bull, Udo resembled a blond troll doll that somebody forced a buzz cut on and then stomped until it stayed permanently squashed. And he looked supremely pissed off about it.

Years later, comedian Patton Oswalt emerged and there was a new go-to in trying to describe how goddamnably odd Udo looked . . . and how that made him, and the music of Accept, all the more awesome.

The band is best known for the single "Balls to the Wall," the video of which climaxes with Udo riding a wrecking ball smack through the titular brick edifice. It's a perfect image for a title that perfectly sums up Accept's sound: heavier and more destructive than even the hardest New Wave of British Heavy Metal bands, inflamed further by an "all in" abandon that would lead directly to thrash.

The speed may not yet have been in place, but the hellhounds-unleashed percussion of drummer Jörg Fischer and Wolf Hoffmann's bone-break guitar crunch directly fueled the thrash tank.

Udo, of course, brought the ugly. Beautifully.

ANTHRAX

Anthrax rocks on any number of counts.

They are, of course, one of thrash's Big Four, as well as one of the curiously few world-class metal bands to originate in New York City (and they come from Queens and the Bronx, at that!).

Anthrax also pioneered rap-metal by way of their better-than-Beasties "I'm the Man," and a visceral mash-up with Public Enemy on "Bring the Noise."

Donning "jam"-style surfer shorts and bent-billed ball caps, Anthrax connected immediately to the primarily punk-driven skater scene.

Punker still, they always publicly worshipped the Ramones and commingled effortlessly with even the most violently unfriendly factions of New York hardcore, even splitting off for the revolutionary crossover stupor-group Stormtroopers of Death (more commonly known, on countless T-shirts and skateboard stickers, as "S.O.D.").

In an amusingly open secret, members of Anthrax also played "incognito" as Dü Hüskers, a Hüsker Dü cover band.

While never garnering the larger glories of Megadeth or the

diabolically devoted congregation of Slayer, let alone the main-stream superstardom of Metallica, Anthrax has persistently moved forward since forming (as did Metallica) in 1981.

Not even 9/11 could stop them. The band was as rattled as any other native New Yorkers following the 2001 World Trade Center attacks, but they then faced wholly unpredictable scrutiny when a series of follow-up terror attempts involved victims being infected with the cattle disease known as, yes, anthrax.

Perhaps most impressive is that Anthrax has triumphed, flour-ished, and persisted while never quite finding the right lead singer.

That's got to be a first for any group, let alone the class clowns of what was once the most brutal mutation of the most evil form of rock 'n' roll.

To date, Anthrax has been through eight vocalists, the best-known being Joey Belladonna, who fronted the band during its most fruitful period, 1985 to 1992, singing on their signature clas-sic album, *Among the Living*.

Belladonna, a poodle-headed belter who looked and sounded like he could have slipped out of the striped spandex of any con-current hair-metal outfit, may well have kept Anthrax from ever receiving the full-on embrace that Metallica got from previously opposed hard rock subcultures.

The human element that did keep Anthrax so largely beloved through the years is their non-singing front-man-on-the-side, gui-tarist and chief songwriter Scott Ian.

Ian defines Anthrax, with his outer-borough attitude, all-encompassing musical interests, and, above all, his wise-guy good humor. And his trademark goatee is the most celebrated facial hair in rock outside of ZZ Top.

Laughter, in fact, is what Anthrax brought to the Big Four's oth-erwise entirely unsmiling (funeral) party. Whereas Metallica, Slayer, and Megadeth fly on fury and resentment, Anthrax caroms about Three Stooges style, gleefully vandalizing the scene with vintage New York cut-uppery stemming from Don-Rickles-era Borscht Belt comedy and later embodied by hairy, scary, pre-Hamptons Howard Stern.

Visual case in point: *Mad* magazine artist Mort Drucker painted the band's portrait for the 1988 cover of *State of Euphoria*.

Then consider how "I'm the Man" is built on a quote from Rodney Dangerfield's 1983 knee-slapper *Easy Money* and includes samples of Sam Kinison (plus an errant flash of "Master of Puppets"). Two minutes in, there's a "Hava Nagila" riff, and the entire rhyme scheme is punctuated by the band failing to rhyme, with one notable exception being a glorious rhyming of "farted" and "retarded." Then they name-check the "anal vapor" of the Mentors' El Duce.

Stormtroopers of Death cuts even looser, with paeans to "Freddy Krueger," "Premenstrual Princess Blues," and "Fist-Banging Mania"; five-second tributes to Jimi Hendrix and "Diamonds and Rust"; and their trademark political-correctness-decimating anthems "Speak English or Die" and "Fuck the Middle East."

In 1992, Anthrax guested on *Married . . . with Children*, injecting thrash into prime time and ending the episode by joining fellow guest Edd "Kookie" Byrnes for an uproariously knuckleheaded a cappella round of his 1969 novelty hit, "Kookie, Kookie, Lend Me Your Comb."

None of this is to paint Anthrax as a joke. The humor, in fact, only solidifies the band's other talents and abilities, adding a unique spice to seriously heavy mix. Also serious is their lifelong bond, in myriad ways, to Metallica.

After jaunting east in 1981 and wearing out their welcome at the New Jersey home of Megaforce Records founders Jon and Marsha Zazula, Metallica moved into Anthrax's practice space, a one-room cold-water hellhole in Queens consisting of musical equipment, beer empties, rat droppings, and discarded foam rubber fashioned into sleep chambers.

Salvation came in the form of Anthrax members allowing the California ragamuffins to shower at their homes, while also being generous with hot dogs, beer, blankets, and companionship.

Thirty years later, Anthrax and Metallica continue to hang out. Notably, they did so when in September 2011, when they bookended a Big Four concert at Yankee Stadium, the first-ever hard rock event in the history of the House That Ruth Built.

Sluggers and pluggers these longtime friends are, onward into the Great Metal Eternal.

DEATH ANGEL

The Osmonds from hell, by way of the Philippines and the early-'80s Bay Area hesher revolution. Unquestionably the greatest family act in the history of thrash, Death Angel took flight in 1982 as four teenage Filipino-American cousins got bit by the headbanging bug and then got great at creating headbanging music.

By mere virtue of their ethnic and family ties, Rob Cavestany (lead guitar), Dennis Pepa (vocals, bass), Gus Pepa (rhythm guitar), and Andy Galeon (drums—fourteen when they started!) certainly looked different from the bulk of their thrash brethren. And if they didn't sound entirely different, they definitely did sound great—so much so that, in 1986, amidst the mania of *Master of Puppets*, Kirk Hammett took time to produce Death Angel's demo, *Kill As One*.

It was strong enough to land an Enigma record deal, and the 1987 debut album *The Ultraviolence* suggested a brimming bundle of energy that would push thrash to new technical complexities, growing more powerful in the process.

Sadly, Death Angel share more than just time, place, and musical history with Metallica: They've also had shit luck with tour vehicles. Severe injuries from a 1991 bus accident broke the band up for a decade.

Death Angel reunited for a 2001 charity gig to benefit Testament singer Chuck Billy's cancer treatment. They played occasionally for the next decade until releasing the fearsomely excellent *Relentless Retribution* and hitting the road with Anthrax and, happily, Testament.

Long may they flap their reclaimed black wings.

DESTRUCTION

They're German, so it's a given that there's a lot of metal along with the heavy when it comes to Destruction. What grabbed the world first, though, was this band's demonic velocity.

Destruction brought the noise on their 1986 breakthrough,

Eternal Devastation. Founding vocalist/bassist Marcel "Schmier" Schirmer, guitarist Mike Sifringer, and drummer Tommy Sandmann powered past all previous power trios and rushed beyond speed metal into an autobahn lane almost all its own.

EXODUS

In thrash, you have the Big Four—Metallica, Slayer, Megadeth, and Anthrax—and, then, thumping and throttling and pummeling and puking and raging up a tsunami-force hell-racket right underneath that most aboveground echelon, you have Exodus.

In many ways, that's actually a step up.

Anger and aggression may define the wellspring from which all thrash draws, but Exodus sank even deeper for inspiration. Their music deals in palpably rendered violence—not occult invocations or sword-and-sorcery fantasia, but real bite-the-curb-and-wait-for-the-boot-stomp carnage.

That's what Exodus sang about, that's how they played it, and that's how it hit audiences upon immediate impact of their 1985 debut, the punk-paced scalp-splitter, *Bonded by Blood*.

"Bang your head against the stage and metal takes it price," roars too-loud-to-live-long vocalist Paul Baloff. "Bonded by blood!"

Oof.

Bonded by Blood, with its notoriously grotesque Siamese twins cover art (one baby looks nice, the other looks like he listens to Exodus), came about after Exodus had solidified its reputation over the previous four years with killer live shows and demos that tore up the heavy metal tape-trading circuit.

Singer Baloff and guitarist Gary Holt formed Exodus in 1981 along with the band's none-too-secret weapon, axe wizard Kirk Hammett. They rose rapidly to the forefront of the combustion-ready Bay Area metal scene, challenged only by Metallica for top-dog status.

Once Metallica split for New Jersey in '82, though, whatever relief Exodus may have enjoyed was short-lived. After Metallica fired Dave Mustaine, Kirk Hammett packed up and headed east to fill the now-open lead guitarist slot.

Still, what bitterness existed, says Hammett, was only "at first. But they understood. If any of them had been approached, they would have done the same thing."

By the mid-'80s, Metallica strode high between *Ride the Lightning* and *Master of Puppets*, so any competition was over. Exodus maintained a dedicated fan base, but they wanted more. Paul Baloff seemed to be an obstacle to bigger-ticket success. Exodus sacrificed him—only to find, ultimately, that his ousting might have been a mistake.

While Accept's Udo Dirkschneider opened the gateway for affably repulsive extreme metal front men, Baloff barreled through right after him, knocking the whole fence down as he rolled forward. With his beer-barrel build and proto-Buzz-Osborne freak-fro, Paul resembled pro wrestling's Wild Samoans, and he sang like those guys fought—viciously, bombastically, and triumphantly. Alas, that's also how Paul Baloff consumed alcohol . . . well, all except for the "triumphantly" part.

In 1987, ex-Testament singer Steve "Zetro" Souza assumed Exodus microphone duties, resulting in the so-so *Pleasures of the Flesh* album and, two years later, the considerably better *Fabulous Disaster*.

More than a footnote, and beloved by their peers and thrash fans everywhere, Exodus has soldiered on through breakups, regroupings, a reunion with Paul Baloff, and even Baloff's stroke-induced death in 2002 at the ripe old age (for him) of forty-one.

Gary Holt remains the sole original member of this still active outfit. As Exodus remains a great live outfit whose records continue to inspire, it's clear that Holt is enough. Exodus is its own promised land.

KREATOR

Essen, Germany's most diabolical post–World War II execution squad, Kreator whipped up a unique form of thrash that matched Slayer for mad intensity and Metallica for tunefulness while raining down walls of dread and evil energy in a distinctly European manner, even on their slapped-together 1985 debut, *Endless Pain*.

As such, Kreator was a considerable influence on the burgeoning forms of black metal and death metal and, being German, their tentacles tickled the entirety of dark-hearted underground cultures everywhere.

Kreator's name slams true.

Pleasure to Kill is Kreator's first big album from, inevitably, 1986. Nineteen eighty-seven's *Terrible Certainty* and 1989's *Extreme Aggression* took the band worldwide—hellacious Huns out for blood and ever more barbaric riffs.

Come the new decade, Kreator figured more or less as the German Metallica, and they faced a challenge similar to that of the American Metallica: Once you've thrashed as hard and as heavy as possible, what do you do next?

Metallica rose to the occasion with the Black Album, while Kreator came up with *Renewal* in 1992, a slowed-down foray into machine rock. Metallica annoyed many fans with their alt-metal rebirth, but they gained legions of new ones in the process. Kreator had no such luck.

Impressively, in a way, Kreator responded to their audience's rejection by experimenting even further over the next decade. Several records have followed, and the band tours with classic thrash outfits such as Exodus and Death Angel to the spine-snapping delight, now, of multiple generations.

Kreator *über alles*.

MEGADETH

The pain of rejection can indeed prove productive, as evidenced by the decades-spanning artistry and multiplatinum abundance of thrash metal superpower Megadeth.

The saga begins in 1982. Guitar warrior Dave Mustaine got unceremoniously fired from Metallica and dumped onto a Greyhound in Times Square. Over the course of the ensuing tortuous four-day journey back to San Francisco, Mustaine opened a political pamphlet on the perils of nuclear arms and read:

"The arsenal of megadeath can't be rid no matter what the peace treaties come to."

And so commenced one man's quixotic campaign first to beat,

then to unseat, and then to merely compete against the preeminent emperors of heavy metal. Mustaine would deem their empire "evil." Metallica themselves might disagree. But then again, maybe not.

Teaming with bassist David "Junior" Ellefson, Mustaine debuted his anti-Metallica squadron Megadeth as soon as humanly possible at Bay Area metal mainstay Ruthie's Inn in 1983. "I had bullet belts and dummy hand grenades on for this show," Mustaine said. "I wanted to make a statement."

The music spoke even louder than the props. Tense and intense, hard and hardcore, Megadeth immediately rushed ahead of the thrash pack and right up to Metallica's battle zone (in time, of course, both bands would comprise half of thrash's Big Four, the other half being Slayer and Anthrax).

When Metallica released *Ride the Lightning* in 1984, Megadeth responded with *Killing Is My Business . . . and Business Is Good!* Two years later, after Metallica issued its masterpiece, *Master of Puppets*, Megadeth put out its own thorny-crowning achievement, *Peace Sells . . . but Who's Buying.*

And so it went, until Megadeth was outpacing Metallica in terms of product (including some excellent records, e.g., 1988's *So Far, So Good . . . So What!*; 1990's *Rust in Peace*; and 1992's *Countdown to Extinction*), but after the Black Album, Metallica became, well, METALLICA.

And then it was game over. But the game kept going.

Extinction counted down to. Only . . . not.

Megadeth continued pumping out albums with diminishing (although never uninteresting or entirely dismissible) returns, while Metallica simply continued Metallicizing.

Who beat who here no longer seems up for debate, but Metallica's place atop the pantheon should not discount Mustaine and Megadeth. Just imagine if Pete Best, upon being told by the Beatles to pack his sticks and let Ringo sit down, had reacted by forming a band on the order of . . . not quite the Stones, but let's say the Who or Pink Floyd.

Such a shadow group's existence and perseverance would be

fascinating in and of itself, but with Megadeth, the quality of the music—ferocious, determined, at times reckless—makes it considerably more engaging.

Of course, that doesn't make the nasty give-and-take between the two camps any less captivating to fans. Mustaine can be classless—boastfully claiming, more than once, that he slept with Hammett's girlfriend prior to getting fired—but his appearance in the documentary *Some Kind of Monster* (2002) vividly hammers home that the rage and regret driving Megadeth's music remains all too real.

Sitting down with Lars Ulrich for the first time in decades, Mustaine confesses: "I've had to watch people around the world talk about what a great guitar player Kirk is, and what a piece of shit I am, and that I got kicked out of Metallica, and I wasn't good enough for them, and that I was a loser. And I have had to deal with that for twenty years. It's been hard, Lars. It's been hard to watch everything that you guys touch turn to gold, and everything I do fuckin' backfire. And I'm sure there's a lot of people that would consider my backfire complete success. Am I happy being number two? No! Do I wish it was 1982 all over again, and you guys woke me up and said, 'Hey, Dave, you need to go to AA'? Yeah. I'd give anything for that chance."

There's no turning back time and for Mustaine, the score may never be settled. His 2010 autobiography, *Mustaine: A Heavy Metal Memoir*, is spiked with barbs and occasional real venom toward members of a band on whose records he never got to play—while he still never really takes what one would call proper pride in the fact that Megadeth has sold more than 15 million albums!

On the upside, the 2011 Big Four stadium shows channeled the triumphs and tragedies of these veterans into a series of flaming pyres of good feelings and future possibilities. For Mustaine and Megadeth, let's hope it's a phoenix moment, and not a Viking funeral.

NUCLEAR ASSAULT

Nuclear Assault is Anthrax's Megadeth—a fired member's "revenge" project that, while never engulfing or surpassing the original outfit, took on a life of its own and can claim a unique slot in the pantheon of thrash at its most monumental.

The ex-Anthraxer in question is bass player Danny Lilker, who was axed after 1983's *A Fistful of Metal*. He met his perfect partner in guitarist and vocalist John Connelly, who had also played with Anthrax, but never even got to record with them.

These men on a mission combined speed metal with hardcore punk and, lyrically, infused Nuclear Assault with social consciousness akin to that of UK crust battalions Discharge and Napalm Death. They predated Metallica's politically aware outbursts with flesh-flaying antiwar diatribes, and commissioned cornea-cracking apocalyptic paintings as cover art.

While Nuclear Assault railed against governmental injustice and corporate slaughter, they never entirely abandoned the wiseass New York humor of their original ensemble ("Butt Fuck," their scabrous ode to Mötley Crüe's Vince Neil and his lethal drunk driving habits, was retitled, after some record company sweating, as "You Figure It Out").

Like their namesake itself, Nuclear Assault flashed out seemingly just as soon as they really seemed to be making an impact. But the fallout is still being felt.

OVERKILL

Not to be confused with SST Records' punk-metal hybrid Overkill L.A. or snazzy-dressed Chicago groovesters Urge Overkill, pure thrash powerhouse Overkill originally hailed, in 1980, from scenic Old Bridge Township, New Jersey.

Whereas their neighbors Bon Jovi took to mall fashion and pop hooks, Overkill proudly patrolled Jersey's gutters. Their angst was the same as Metallica's on the West Coast, while their hard-knock, outside-NYC sensibility matched that of Anthrax over in Queens. These were T-shirts, torn jeans, and high-top sneakers dudes, dressed to impress you only with the might of their sound.

The band initially performed Ramones and Dead Boys covers as Virgin Killer (naming themselves after a Scorpions album), before adding Judas Priest and Riot songs to the set and changing their names from the Lubricunts to Overkill (after a Motörhead album). That's as fine a list of ingredients as any recipe in the thrash kitchen, and, following their heavily traded 1983 demo *Power in Black*, Overkill really got cooking.

A self-titled 1984 EP garnered Overkill a contract with Metallica's original label, Megaforce, in 1985, followed by two years of touring with Anthrax and Megadeth, and 1987's *Fuck You* (whose cover was adorned by a flying middle finger).

Overkill also, in the form of winged-skull mascot "Chaly," created thrash's best-loved graphic logo. Chaly might not match Iron Maiden's Eddie, but hey, he's from Jersey. And that means a lot.

PANTERA

The 1980s were full of scene-defining, larger-than-loudness metal bands. But as Anthrax's Scott Ian points out on VH1's *Top 100 Greatest Artists of Hard Rock*, "In the '90s, there was only one band. Pantera."

Ironically, these future era-defining badasses prowled out of Arlington, Texas, all the way back in 1983, initially under the guise of mascara-plastered hair-glamsters Pantera's Metal Magic (the goofiest name this side of, yes, Metallica).

Seven years, four zippo-impact albums, and a severe lead-singer upgrade later, Pantera issued *Cowboys from Hell* in 1990, careening in off the thrash tsunami and frantically fronted by New Orleans pit bull Phil Anselmo.

This, now, was Pantera fully formed.

In the manner that Metallica pounded punk into metal nearly a decade earlier, Pantera incorporated the '80s' other renegade street music into their freshly ferocious jackhammer riffs and power beats: rap.

This was not the hippity-hoppity rap-metal to come; rather, Anselmo's hellhound barks perfectly top guitarist Dimebag Darrell Abbott's jagged, deceptively minimalist guitar blasts (leading into lusciously downpouring solos) and the megaton rhythm charge of drummer Vinnie Paul (Darrell's brother) and bassist Rex Brown. The sound is vast and constricted at once. It hits like a thousand fists. It is Pantera—and only Pantera.

Throughout the high alt-rock Lollapalooza era, Pantera performed with Metallica in Moscow and produced four classic albums. *Far Beyond Driven* even debuted at #1 on the *Billboard* chart in 1994, two weeks before Kurt Cobain shot himself.

In addition to his vocal styling and unprecedented knuckle-sandwich stage presence, Anselmo proved to be a wild card on par, in terms of eclectic taste, with Metallica's Cliff Burton.

His subsequent and side projects attest to this. Consider such Anselmo endeavors as sludge gods Down (with Pepper Keenan, who almost replaced Jason Newsted in Metallica), blackened groovers Superjoint Ritual (with Hank Williams III), and hardcore punkers Arson Anthem (again, weirdly, with Hank Williams III).

Alas, tragedy stalked this band like few others. Anselmo's five-alarm heroin addiction and the onstage murder of Dimebag Darrell by a psychotic "fan" in 2003 have forever mired Pantera in too-true human horror.

Although they arose too late to qualify alongside Metallica, Slayer, Megadeth, and Anthrax, the true lasting legacy of Pantera proves that here, there is no shame in placing fifth.

POSSESSED

Similar to the way Venom announced a new genre with their title "Black Metal," San Francisco pioneers Possessed debuted in 1984 with the demo *Death Metal*.

The four songs (including the title track) that originally appeared on that grinding glimpse of a particularly foreboding future made it the following year to *Seven Churches*, Possessed's—and death metal's—first album.

It was an instant underground must-have comprised of satanic summoning and Drano-gargling calls to slaughter peeled off at vicious velocity by way of sumptuous musicianship worthy of the record's mysterious name. The blast beats, the demonic obsession and, most especially, the vomit-growl vocals of all future death metal arrived first on *Seven Churches*. Thrash bashed anew—unto death.

By any standard, *Seven Churches* is a shocker. To know that it was the work of drunken San Francisco sixteen-year-olds who had to schedule practices and performing around their high school classes makes it nothing short of a decidedly godless miracle.

Darker and more alarming is that the Possessed of *Seven Churches* was born of real-life teen suicide. The band's original singer, Barry Fisk, shot himself to death at sixteen. This prompted founders Mike Torrao (guitars) and Mike Sus (drums) to invite singing bass player Jeff Becerra and guitarist Larry Lalonde to leave their hard rock garage outfit Blizzard and fill the void.

"I wanted to go heavier [than Blizzard] anyway," recalls Becerra. "I was more into being heavy as far as drinking beer, going out with as many girls as I could, and playing as fast and heavy as I could, like Motörhead. I asked Mike what the name of the band was and he said, 'Possessed.' I said it sounded kind of satanic and he said, 'Well, it is!' That was kind of scary."

Debbie Abono, a legendarily hustling manager in Bay Area metal who happened to be the mother of Larry Lalonde's girlfriend, took these high school devil worshippers under her matronly wing, getting Possessed on bills with Metallica, Slayer, and Venom. She also elicited from them, somehow, the masterpiece *Seven Churches*.

"We recorded the albums on Easter vacation," Lalonde says, "so I didn't miss any school."

Roadrunner Records released the album to immediate acclaim, and Possessed spent their 1986 Thanksgiving break in Montreal, playing alongside Celtic Frost, Destruction, Nasty Savage, and Voivod. Remember, this was all before their senior prom!

As to the coinage of "death metal," Becerra says: "I came up with that during an English class in high school. I figured speed metal and black metal were already taken, so what the fuck? So I said death metal because that word wasn't associated with Venom or anybody else. We were trying to be the heaviest thing on the planet. We wanted just to piss people off and send everybody home. And that can't be, like, flower metal."

Stunningly mature logic like that aside, Possessed were still a pack of kids and they screwed up everything but the release date of their second album, *Beyond the Gates* (it dropped on Halloween

1986), a bummer collapse into standard thrash after their genre-creating premier.

Who cares? Possessed captured on record the sound of adolescent American heshers inventing a newly barbarous extreme art form.

SEPULTURA

Brazil's most sensory-overloading export prior to the advent of contemporary waxing procedures and/or Joey Silvera she-male porn, Sepultura (Portuguese for "grave") forced thrash forward into death metal and political anger—rages born not of collegiate theory or privileged guilt, but from growing up under a totalitarian regime where getting caught with the wrong metal or punk record could easily get you "disappeared."

That is some heavy shit. And that's how Sepultura plays it.

Headbanging teenage brothers Max and Igor Cavalera (on vocals and drums, respectively) created Sepultura in 1984, and the band's evolution was a slow burn, matching Brazil's own mid-'80s emergence from twenty years of savage military dictatorship.

Sepultura took flight just after thrash peaked, with 1987's *Schizophrenia* and 1989's *Beneath the Remains*. As the '90s dawned and thrash gave way to grunge and pop-punk, Sepultura dug in and got hairier and scarier, delivering the death metal milestone *Arise* as an extreme counterbalance to Metallica's Black Album in 1991.

Two years later, Sepultura's hardcore punk and industrial-influenced masterpiece *Chaos AD* essentially forged the groove-metal blueprint that Pantera would perfect shortly thereafter.

The experimental *Roots* proved even more beloved among fans and critics in 1996—no small feat for a decade during which metal was largely forced underground.

Family tragedy and management disputes prompted front man Max Cavalera to quit Sepultura at this creative and commercial peak. He formed the popular Soulfly (one of the groove metal greats), while his old band has trudged on with Cleveland-bred vocalist Derrick Green manning the mic.

Since the schism, the most noteworthy project by Sepultura proper has been a Brazilian Volkswagen commercial wherein the band played bossa nova and the announcer proclaimed, "It's the first time you've seen Sepultura like this. And a sedan like this one too!"

In 2009, even Igor Cavalera hung up his drumsticks.

Still, the name and the essential catalogue of Sepultura will remain among the most revered in heavy metal forever. In January 2010, the group opened for Metallica at a São Paulo soccer stadium, performing in front of more than 100,000 admirers. That may say a lot about brand recognition, but it says even more about headbangers' reverence for their own musical history.

SLAYER

Pure evil.

Other bands may now surpass Slayer in terms of "extreme" sounds or lyrics, but nobody before or since has connected so singularly and so unflinchingly to the blackest pits of life's deepest-buried hurts and hatreds—theirs and ours alike.

In fact, to go "beyond" Slayer in pursuit of savagery, one passes out of relatable rock music into the cartoony showboat antics of Marilyn Manson, the Cookie Monster grumbles of death metal, the tinny dentist-drill dynamics of black metal, or the busted TV static of power electronics, wherein fanciful sadists like Whitehouse mix rants about butt rape with samples of weeping moms mourning murdered toddlers.

Each can be effective in its way, but their appeal is narrowcast, to say the least. Slayer conjures demons we all share, by way of music that naturally speaks to (and for) the same audience as Metallica—which is to say, everybody.

That's not to say, however, that everybody is (or has ever been) prepared to handle Slayer—even, sometimes, Metallica.

Popular legend has it that Southern California's scariest began life as Dragonslayer, named for the 1981 Disney movie, but guitarist Kerry King adamantly insists it's not true. Slayer did, however, initially wield pentagrams, face paint, and other established metal tropes that they'd eventually either phase out or drop entirely as the thrash aesthetic became codified.

Slayer's satanic invocations, in fact, got them guff from the more gutter-realistic Metallica early on, as did a quantum leap in speed after the two bands played together.

Show by show, album by album, these two outlaw outfits that were inevitably—and correctly—lumped together aimed to out-gun one another until 1986, the year thrash broke, when Metallica let loose *Master of Puppets* in March and Slayer retaliated three weeks before Halloween with *Reign in Blood*.

Master of Puppets would come to be regarded one of rock's all-time great albums, but *Reign in Blood* remains the pinnacle of extreme metal.

Commencing with a chillingly nonjudgmental rundown of atrocities perpetrated by Nazi *schweinhund* Dr. Josef Mengele on "Angel of Death," *Reign in Blood* tears through ten intricately formed, lethally executed songs in a punk-paced twenty-eight minutes and fifty-six seconds. It all builds to an inescapable boil until "Raining Blood," a chronicle of a damned soul storming heaven to overthrow the Power That Is, explodes in a strobe-lit apocalypse of godless racket and, yes, the sound of what is presumably red rain falling.

And there it was. The end of metal. Slayer hit it first and fastest and loudest and best. In one way, that's a definitive triumph, but in another, it's a burden and a bitch because, since you can't stop, where do you go after that?

Reign in Blood, in fact, painted Slayer into a crimson-hued corner the likes of which Metallica never had to deal with. For example, Metallica followed *Master of Puppets* with *Garage Days Re-Revisited*, a scrappy covers collection that enabled them to introduce new bassist Jason Newsted and regroup before taking the next step up. Slayer, having reached the end of all possible evil metal, could only try to do it again, only, somehow, differently.

For 1988's *South of Heaven*, guitarist Jeff Hanneman told *Decibel* magazine: "We knew we couldn't top *Reign in Blood*, so we had to slow down. We knew whatever we did was gonna be compared to that album, and I remember we actually discussed slowing down. It was weird." Weird, and disappointing, it turned out, prompting

Slayer to hit the gas again for *Seasons in the Abyss* in 1990, to better effect.

Come the next decade, though, Metallica would be, well, Metallica and Slayer would be . . . less Slayer.

Relieved of trying to one-up Metallica, Slayer has continued on to extreme metal godhood, selling out arenas and issuing consistently worthwhile albums.

They even pulled a *Garage Days* move in 1996 by way of their punk covers collection *Undisputed Attitude*. Amusingly, their version of Minor Threat's "Guilty of Being White" incensed creator Ian MacKaye, who intended it as an anti-racism screed and suspected sarcasm in Slayer's approach, particularly when vocalist Tom Araya (a dusky-skinned Chilean) ends it by singing, "Guilty of being right." Groused McKaye: "That is so offensive to me." Metallica never got such grief from Glenn Danzig.

Ace performances and affable personalities keep Slayer beloved among the loveless. At no point in the past thirty years has the band not figured prominently in any discussion of contemporary metal. Few other groups in any other genre can claim such long-standing significance—let alone so brutally.

Today Slayer plays routinely with Metallica, and when they tour on their own, their taste in opening acts regularly defines the cream of whatever is the given era's new metal crop. Among more recent examples have been Cradle of Filth, Children of Bodom, In Flames, Machine Head, Mastodon, Trivium, and Amon Amarth.

So while Metallica moves freely about the daylit sphere of worldwide superstardom, Slayer remains their most direct pipeline into the metal's ongoing pitch-black night. They function not so much now as the "top" half of metal's Big Four, but more as a yin and yang—or, more accurately, a yang and yanger—of hard rock's outermost reaches.

Long may they reign. In blood. Yours, mine, and everybody's.

S.O.D. (STORMTROOPERS OF DEATH)

Venom first took on the mantle of "punks with long hair," and Metallica made the crossover even more perceptible in its music.

But the true "God*damn*—there it *is!*" moment of the once-and-forever punk-metal crossover occurs with the (all the way) down-tuned, forward-surging riff of "March of the S.O.D."

The first track on *Speak English or Die* by Stormtroopers of Death—known more commonly as S.O.D.—makes clear that we have marched into a new epoch of epicness.

Intended as a one-off Anthrax side lark, S.O.D. is comprised of Scott Ian on guitar, Charlie Benante on drums, Dan Lilker (originally of Anthrax, then of Nuclear Assault) playing bass, and, manhandling the microphone, primate-proportioned Anthrax roadie Billy Milano.

S.O.D.'s *Speak English or Die*, recorded in three days, served as a sudden rallying point among both hardcore baldies and metalhead long-locks. The initial rush job benefits the material. The album is off-the-cuff without being sloppy, intense without being a downer, and (the neatest feat of all) gut-busting without being a joke. And "politically incorrect" does not begin to do it (in)justice.

While unimaginable today, even in 1985 titles like "Speak English or Die" and "Fuck the Middle East" made proper-thinking citizens uncomfortable, as did lyrics such as those in "The Ballad of Jimi Hendrix" (five seconds long, consisting entirely of "He's dead!").

Among S.O.D.'s most ardent boosters was Metallica. Here was East Coast brazenness and bravado beyond what San Francisco, even in the darkness-driven thrash scene, could possibly permit. Hunter, gun nut, and gearhead James Hetfield was an especially big fan.

Speak English or Die proved to be a record that will never die. Fourteen years later, S.O.D. reunited for their only studio follow-up to date, *Bigger Than the Devil* (standout tracks include "Kill the Assholes," "Free Dirty Needles," "Celtic Frosted Flakes" and posthumous tributes to Phil Hartman and Michael Hutchence as respectful as you'd imagine). It, too, is great, as are the band's live releases and a 2002 tour documentary, *Kill Yourself: The Movie.*

Three generations of hard rockers have now heeded this gnarly, endlessly influential, impossible-to-keep-together crew's advice, killing themselves to rock—through music, through fearlessness, through keeping tongues in their cheeks instead of up the Man's *tuchus*—just like Stormtroopers of Death.

SODOM

If you're going for an unholy moniker, you can take the overt shock route (Anal Cunt and Rotting Christ provide two luminous examples) or you can go biblical, as did Germany's Sodom, naming themselves for the city whose sexual abominations so infuriated the Lord that he smote it in a feces-fit of fire and brimstone.

Rib-tickling gay connotations aside (which they probably never considered anyway), calling your band Sodom is one hell of a way to take the piss right out of the Old Testament's poop-pipe.

The stage names of the original lineup are similarly bold-stroked: Tom Angelripper, Bloody Monster, Arius Blasphemer, and Aggressor. Mr. Monster was replaced early on by Christian "Witch-hunter" Dudek.

The most Venom-blackened of Deutschland's "Three Kings" (Destruction and Kreator donned the other two crowns), Sodom further merged thrash and death metal into a wicked, fittingly decadent sound that was also German above all (*über alles?*).

Willfully villainous English-as-a-second-language adds charm to Sodom's most intentionally evil numbers.

That lyrical clunkiness does not diminish the aesthetic success of Sodom, however; in fact, it enhances it. These German ne'er-do-wells took to stages and studios hell-bent on conjuring visceral dark mayhem and that, for sure, they made happen.

That old black (metal) magic cast a spell on everybody.

TESTAMENT

Brawny Berkeley bashers Testament moshed out of the same Bay Area thrash pond that spawned Metallica, squalling and brawling toward the top of the class by the end of the '80s.

The three albums Testament issued during the metal decade's final three years—*The Legacy*, *New Order*, and *Practice What You Preach*—define the sound and the scene as much as any other contenders.

The omnipresent Testament patches, stickers, and graffiti covering any place that metal was played did not occur simply because the band turned their name into a cool logo (which, like Metallica, they did).

Metallica's early success proved an immediate boon to Testament as the latter signed to Megaforce Records and took to the road in support of Anthrax (both being crucial forces in the establishment of Metallica).

The energy, vitality, and instantly identifiable spin that Testament put on thrash, of course, hurled them forward more so than mere professional connections. In that circle, at the moment, it wasn't whom you knew, it was how hard you got heads banging.

Leading the throw down was formidable front-force Chuck Billy, a massive presence in every sense. Toweringly tall and shaped like a steel-working Sasquatch, Billy bellowed Leviathan style while Alex Skolnick (on guitar) and Greg Christian (on bass) whipped up an appropriately biblical-proportioned temple of noise behind him.

Ultimately, the crucial run of Testament aped the thrash song template—speedy, furious, cramming intense and complex twists and turns into segments that fly by in a flash and then, suddenly, are over.

To its credit, the band has never broken up, and survived even Chuck Billy's bleak cancer bout in the early 2000s. They also pull no punches when it comes to calling Metallica on the carpet.

Chuck Billy first criticized James Hetfield's performance on *Load*. He's quoted in the book *James Hetfield: The Wolf at Metallica's Door* as saying: "When I heard that record it sounded to me like it wasn't him. It wasn't the James that I knew. There was none of the clever lyrics and clever parts. It changed how I felt about their music."

Hetfield later confessed that he agreed, telling EddieTrunk.com, "Lars and Kirk were into abstract art, pretending they were gay. I think they knew it bugged me. I just went along with the makeup and all the stupid, crazy shit they felt they needed to do. Image is not an evil thing, but if the image is not you then it doesn't make much sense. I yanked at least half of the pictures that were to be in the booklet. It all went against what I was feeling."

Alex Skolnick went even further in reaction to *St. Anger*, writing on his website: "When I heard ['St. Anger'] on the radio, we were all in disbelief. There is no unity or cohesiveness to the songs. Some of them are downright funny, as if *Saturday Night Live* was doing a skit making fun of them. This album represents what they are now: a sloppy mess (albeit one with a lot of wealth and power). Lars Ulrich once said that Bon Jovi's music represents everything wrong with the music business. The same can now be said of Metallica."

Harsh words, but they came from a place of truth. Metallica never directly responded, but they did go on to come back, hard, in 2008, with *Death Magnetic*. And that speaks volumes.

Metal sharpens metal.

THE GOD THAT FAILED
Guns N' Roses

For a while, it seemed a sure bet that Guns N' Roses would reign forever as the biggest hard rock band in the history of both hardness and rock.

The five-piece ragamuffin regiment leapt to life in 1985 from the same Sunset Strip scene that Metallica had abandoned for more northern climes.

Fronted by sensitive Indiana banshee W. Axl Rose and single-named, biracial axe-master Slash, Guns N' Roses' lineup also bespoke influences beyond mere metal.

Rhythm guitarist Izzy Stradlin was a southern-rock-meets-Carnaby-Street dandy; drummer Steven Adler raged as a crash-and-burn barnstormer in the Keith Moon mold; and bassist Duff McKagan came from Seattle power-poppers the Fastbacks and hardcore punk semi-legends the Fartz.

Their influences ran largely the same as Metallica's, but Guns N' Roses wore theirs on their sleeves (or, in the singer's case, on their headbands).

In August 1987, Metallica followed up the previous year's game-changing *Master of Puppets* LP with *Garage Days Re-Revisited*, an EP of eclectic covers that got down and dirty while simultaneously communicating universe-conquering ambitions.

That same summer, however, also brought with it Guns N' Roses' major label debut, *Appetite for Destruction*. In a single album, GNR appeared to pull off everything Metallica had done to that point, but one better—*Appetite for Destruction* literally charmed the pants off the ladies.

Pondering the lyrics of GNR's breakthrough hit "Sweet Child O' Mine," with its reference to hiding from the thunder in your beloved's warm, safe hair, one commentator remarked: "Those are the kind of words fourteen-year-old girls can relate to. Those are the kind of words fourteen-year-old girls WRITE!"

No one was going to ever confuse the pen of James Hetfield with one belonging to a female high-school freshman.

And so, by the time Metallica released . . . *And Justice for All* in 1988—produced by Mike Clink, who had overseen the recording of *Appetite for Destruction*—Guns N' Roses had clearly surpassed them.

But not forever.

The Year of Our Rock 1991 represented a sea change. Not the least of the tidal waves came from *Metallica* by Metallica and *Use Your Illusion Volumes 1* and *2* by Guns N' Roses.

So as the very nature of rock acclimated itself to precisely what these twin titans had always hoped it would be, the time was at hand for them to compete head-to-head.

Two bands entered the Biggest Hard Rock Band of All Time thunderdome in 1991, and one band left. Since you're reading a book titled *If You Like Metallica . . .* , you already know who it was.

Guns N' Roses' catalytic role in pushing Metallica to aim as high as high was crucial. Lars Ulrich, in particular, became obsessed with GNR upon hearing *Appetite*'s first single, "It's So Easy" (declared the drummer: "It blew my fuckin' head off!").

Use Your Illusion followed Metallica to #1 on the album charts by a week, and by the following summer, the bands had launched a tour together. Metallica played first, by mere dint of Axl Rose's routine practice of taking the stage hours late (if at all).

The globe-mangling rock 'n' roll circus that resulted was a continuous cluster bomb of excess and disasters. James Hetfield nearly lost his arm to a third-degree burn. Lars got a taste of the "white leather" rock god life and could never look back. Axl broke down, blew up, ignited riots, and never reemerged whole.

While *Metallica* incensed vast seas of old-school Metallica admirers, it won the band even vaster seas of new devotees. In contrast, the two-purchases-required *Use Your Illusion* experience proved to be an initial rush followed by disillusionment for Guns N' Roses fans—as well as for Guns N' Roses.

Axl coped with post-*Illusion* stress disorder by swiping a move from the Metallica playbook. Guns N' Roses rush out a collection of punk covers.

Nineteen ninety-three's *The Spaghetti Incident?*—the last recording with the essential GNR lineup—came off as cheap (although, to be sure, they did not insist, as Metallica had on their EP cover, that you not pay more than $5.99 for it) and easy. From there, Axl transformed into the rubber-mugged, cornrow-headed Howard Hughes of rock.

You know what Metallica did. You're soaking in it.

DEATH MAGNETIC
Death Metal

As scary as Black Sabbath was in 1970 and as much as Slayer (among others) intensified that fear factor in the '80s, death metal was a whole new dimension in sonic horror.

Avalanche-fast guitars, double-bass-drum blast beats, and repulsive lyrics not so much sung as fire-barfed through a Cookie Monster growl that's anything but crunchy, let alone sweet. Welcome to hell. Welcome to death metal.

Perhaps drawing from the area's hellacious heat, death metal roared to life from Florida, with self-scarred barbarians in sweatpants wrecking frets and splintering countless drumsticks in rampant pursuit of the last-rites brutality.

The Death Metal Dozen (or So)

Atheist—*Unquestionable Presence*
Brutal Truth—*Need to Control*
Cannibal Corpse—*Butchered at Birth, Tomb of the Mutilated*
Carcass—*Heartwork, Necrotism: Descanting the Insalubrious*
Cynic—*Focus*
Death—*Scream Bloody Gore*
Deicide—*Deicide, Legion, Once Upon the Cross*
Dismember—*Indecent and Obscene*
Morbid Angel—*Blessed Are the Sick*
Mortician—*Hacked Up for the Barbecue*
Napalm Death—*Scum, From Enslavement to Obliteration, Fear Emptiness Despair*
Necrophagia—*Season of the Dead*
Obituary—*Slowly We Rot, The End Complete*
Possessed—*Seven Churches*

Rob Zombie. (Photofest)

6

RELOAD:
ALTERNATIVE METAL

Metallica created the genre alternative metal. Point-blank.
While other artists had been tinkering and whipping up the formula since at least Frank Zappa's post-Mothers output—think, for example, of the Butthole Surfers, Fishbone, Jesus Lizard, Godflesh—it was Metallica's complete dominance of '80s underground rock, in all its forms, that bulldozed headlong into the inevitable mainstream of the alt-metal '90s.

Commencing the era with their 10-million-selling Black Album, Metallica's old-school fans spitefully deemed their discarded heroes "Alternica" (and that was even before the haircuts).

Separated now by time, Metallica's move into the alternative arena resulted in the band reverberating through every rock subgenre of the past twenty years.

They defiantly expanded the barriers of what made metal heavy, and empowered every subsequent new dispatch of headbangers to dive in with their own approach.

The bands listed here are direct descendants. Long may future generations prosper and multiply—alternatively.

ALICE IN CHAINS
Unique among Seattle grunge stars, Alice in Chains emanated not from punk, but almost entirely from the same leaden mist that produced Emerald City thrash-masters Metal Church and the Accused.

Johnny Bacolas, bassist of the band Sleze, which would evolve into Alice in Chains, tells of instantly bonding with vocalist Layne Staley over super-hard metal bands: Slayer, Venom, and Armored Saint, to be exact.

What punk did seep into Alice in Chains got there through Crüe and other '80s glam bands who aped Steve Jones's Sex Pistols guitar sound. One group, in fact, is most frequently invoked when talk turns to the band's early ascendance.

"Their first demo probably owed a little bit more to Poison than the huge monster they became," says Soundgarden's Kim Thayil in the grunge history book *Everybody Loves Our Town*. "That really changed after they heard us."

Simply being of the time and place that birthed Nirvana and Pearl Jam may have gotten Alice in Chains branded "grunge." Having Chris Cornell and Mudhoney's Mark Arm appear on the song "Right Turn" certainly pointed toward the *g*-word as well.

Yet something about Alice in Chains has never meshed fully with grungeness.

Slipknot drummer Joey Jordison puts it directly: "Alice in Chains was always a metal band in hiding, with a grunge umbrella."

Guitarist Jerry Cantrell's leads scream metal (including on their *Unplugged* collection), but his unpredictable songwriting choices and gripping harmonies with Staley rendered something genuinely new—something that could take over the world in the wake of Metallica's Black Album. Which it did.

For the first half of the '90s, as grunge flamed up and out and Metallica continually erupted, Alice in Chains created their own niche in the newly expanded universe of MTV and FM radio possibilities.

Every album they released proved to be a classic and every hit single sounded different from the previous one, but, just a few notes in, each song was unmistakably Alice in Chains.

Such success proved too much—as it so often does for many— for Layne Staley, who unofficially left Alice in Chains in 1996 and then all-too-officially left the planet in 2002, succumbing to a heroin and cocaine addiction.

The records live on, not just in and of themselves, but in the way Alice in Chains pushed hard rock forward. And not the least of their beneficiaries is Metallica.

DINOSAUR JR.

What makes Dinosaur Jr. "metal" is the guitar playing of J. Mascis—a fat, filthy Neil Young bowel-belch sound by way of K. K. Downing cannonade and Frank Zappa elasticity.

What makes Dinosaur Jr. decidedly "alternative metal" are the vocals of J. Mascis—a cough-syrup sleepwalk whinny of his own drooping creation.

"Grunge" probably best tags this Amherst, Massachusetts, squad led by Mascis, but metal has always been the tar pit housing this three-headed monster. "We loved speed metal," bassist Lou Barlow said of the group's genesis in Michael Azerrad's indie-rock chronicle *Our Band Could Be Your Life*, "and we loved wimpy-jangly stuff." (Shades of Cliff Burton's devotion to R.E.M.)

Before they were even called Dinosaur (the "Jr." was added under legal duress from a 1960s outfit of the same name), they were Deep Wound, a speed-record-liquefying punk platoon who proved crucial in bridging hardcore to death metal.

Dinosaur released a self-titled debut in 1985. Their masterstroke, *You're Living All Over Me*, came two years later. *Bug!* happened in 1988. That string of albums forced alternative rock—then defined by MTV's Sunday late-night show *120 Minutes*, where Euro-neuters like Yaz and Echo and the Bunnymen were as hard it got—to accept aggressive, guitar-fueled heavy music.

Most immediately thereafter, Nirvana reaped that reward, but so too, in time, did Metallica.

Lou Barlow quit Dinosaur Jr. before their 1990 *Green Mind* album, and founded Sebadoh and Folk Implosion, two bands that, if you like Metallica, odds are you most definitely will not like.

Mascis shepherded Dinosaur Jr. to a bona fide FM radio/prime-time MTV hit in 1994 ("Feel the Pain"). Three years and one more lackluster album later, he retired the band's name.

In 2005, Mascis and Barlow, along with Bonham-mighty drummer Murph, reunited, and Dinosaur Jr. has remained active ever since. Two thousand seven's *Beyond* is very good. Two thousand nine's *Farm* is great.

Between and beyond those records, Barlow continues with Sebadoh, while Mascis helms an array of side projects. Of those, the Boston doom supergroup Upsidedown Cross is headbangingly amusing, while the stoner rock shamans Witch are creating some of the most vital retro-metal now happening. Mascis plays drums in both, as though that's what he'd been doing all along.

FAITH NO MORE

A year or so before the Black Album and Nirvana's *Nevermind*, San Francisco freak-funk art-metal marauders Faith No More softened MTV and FM radio obstacles for the coming heaviosity by way of "Epic," their slow-soaring, half-rapped hard rock curiosity that not only made good on its name but also provided a synonym for "awesome" that (thank you, Internet) just won't quit.

FNM had been conducting their whack-rock experiments for nearly a decade prior to *The Real Thing*, the 1989 album that delivered "Epic"—both the single and its iconic dying-fish-flopping video.

The band's only previous semi-hit was "We Care a Lot" in 1985, a bass-popping dance-metal hybrid spotlighting cross-dressing singer Chuck Moseley leading the titular chant in a way that's cool enough so that you really can't tell whether or not he (and by extension the band) means it.

The sarcasm factor increased infinitely upon the institution of Chuck's replacement, Mike Patton of the avant-garde fart-jazz squad Mr. Bungle.

FNM racked up a few lesser party staples (including a note-for-note cover of "Easy" by the Commodores) and opened up on the Metallica/Guns N' Roses stadium tour in 1992.

Seemingly too weird to stay popular, but not strange enough to expand their cult, FNM split up mid-decade and Patton reinvented himself as modern metal's closest equivalent of Frank Zappa.

Any of Patton's many present projects bear investigation, especially his Native American heavy metal ensemble Tomahawk, and Fantômas, his monster-rock collective with the Melvin's Buzz Osborne that reworks movie and cartoon themes as noxious blasts of roaring insanity.

And I tell you this because, really, I care a lot.

HELMET

Gap-teed shorthairs from the early-'90s NYC sewer bubble that belched forth the more industrial Unsane, Prong, and Cop Shoot Cop, Helmet brought a lot of Sabbath to the pissed-off party, courtesy of the Iommi-like lead guitar of Page Hamilton. That's also Page on the Ozzy-like lead vocals.

Helmet head Hamilton arrived at metal after a stint in art racketeers Band of Susans, and his riffs proved solid and salable. Helmet, in fact, scored the first highly publicized post-Nirvana heavy rock cash-in, as they signed to Interscope for a million of what that baby is swimming after on the cover of *Nevermind*.

Beavis and Butt-Head were also sold instantly on Helmet, growling along and throwing horns to the opening crunch of "Unsung" on their show. Observes Beavis: "That drummer looks like a regular guy." Adds Butt-Head: "If you, like, saw these guys on the street, you wouldn't even know they were cool!"

Any remaining doubters after that (and how could there be?) need only listen to any random Helmet release to concur, or you can cut right to the "Motorbreath" cover on the tribute album *Metallic Attack*, where Hamilton teams with Scott Ian to pay proper Big Rotten Apple respect to their Bay Area brethren.

JANE'S ADDICTION

Somewhere in the middle of the 1980s, Perry Farrell saw the future. He was going to be a big part of it, and so, too, was Metallica.

The second part presumably wilted his dreadlocks, seeing how four longhairs from San Francisco singing antiwar anthems would prove too brutish and macho and openly ambitious for his Hollywood Boulevard junkie hustler hippie gentility that fired up (and raked it in from) traveling alt-rock money machine Lollapalooza.

But nobody ever claimed Perry Farrell—recently the highest-profile male cast member of the E! reality TV show *Rock Star Wives*—wasn't one canny fuck. That's why his band Jane's Addiction got its kick from the heavy metal tumult initially whipped up by—who else?—Metallica.

The thing, though, is that Jane's Addiction (aping the malady for which it was named) initially worked. And it stayed that way for a while. *Nothing's Shocking* in 1988 and *Ritual de lo Habitual* in 1990 pretty heavily shook the world and undeniably expanded the language of heavy metal.

Paired in nonstop MTV rotation with Faith No More's "Epic," Jane's "Been Caught Stealing" video delivered the first cracks in the dams of pop culture and mass media sufficiently enough for Nirvana to dynamite the rest open and Metallica to sail in behind them.

Yes, Farrell created Lollapalooza as a vehicle for Jane's Addiction in 1991 and, yes, five years later he turned up his perpetually powdered-on-the-inside-nose at it over the announcement of Metallica as headliners.

Regardless, Farrell and Lilliputian sex-bat guitarist Dave Navarro expanded the perimeters with some freakishly bold hard rock that made Metallica's ultimate triumphs not only possible but, likely, inevitable.

That, and Navarro hosted the CBS game show *Rock Star Supernova* in 2006 costarring Jason Newsted as a judge, and everybody involved has to live with that. Including us. Come on, you can admit you watched it.

KORN

Rock snobs rushed to pooh-pooh the late-'90s/early-2000s "nu-metal" movement, and the relatively short-lived, big-selling blend of hip-hop, alt-rock, and metal guitars does invite reflexive disdain, not the least of which derives from poster mooks Limp Bizkit simply being Limp Bizkit.

But in defense of the backward-red-Yankee-capped throngs, nu-metal did connect with millennial misfits in much the manner that thrash had connected with kids a decade and a half earlier. Whereas Metallica incorporated punk to their heaviness, nu-metal sucked up and hurled back rap, techno, and exploding Internet technology among its metal.

And it gave us Korn.

As Alice Cooper put it on VH1's *100 Greatest Artists of Hard Rock*: "Korn is the new generation metal band. They're half funk, they're half rap, they're all energy."

Jason Newsted agreed on the same show, adding "They're real people and they really love playing real music. Every night they play one-hundred-and-ten percent. They're not going through the motions in any way."

The Bakersfield, California, foursome has struck gold repeatedly since its 1994 debut, even guest-starring on *South Park* in 1999 and, that ultimate rarity for a metal band, playing on *Saturday Night Live* in 2005 (Metallica only got on *SNL* once, in 1997, accompanied by Marianne Faithfull, and they haven't been asked back since).

Front man Jonathan Davis's freaky obscene-phone-caller beat-box histrionics serve as a serious metal touchstone for an entire age group of hard rock disciples. His voice matches (and leads) the energy of musicians behind him, and of the polyglot time from which it arose. Millions of messed-up kids could identify, and again, heavy music moshed onward.

There's certainly nothing corny about that.

MACHINE HEAD

Their name comes from the classic 1972 Deep Purple album (yes, the one with "Smoke on the Water" and "Highway Star" and "Space Truckin'"); their sound comes from all known forms of metal past and present; and the band itself comes from Metallica's hometown of San Francisco.

Machine Head comes with all the parts for a monstrous mechanical animal.

Debuting in 1994, the absolute nadir for metal in mainstream American consciousness, Machine Head's *Burn My Eyes* set Europe ablaze with iron riffs and sheets of bludgeon perfectly bridging the recent past of Pantera and Alice in Chains to the even more technical blitzkriegs to come.

Machine Head picked up an opening slot on the next Slayer tour as a result, and a hard rock dynasty was born.

The More Things Change, the 1997 follow-up LP, makes good on its title, branching out into atmospheric spookery and flighty prog, but 1999's *The Burning Red* is Machine Head's true before-and-after line. New fans thought the record burned, indeed, while old-timers largely saw red.

Just as Metallica cut their hair and headlined Lollapalooza in the second half of the grunge decade, Machine Head rolled with the post-grunge punches smack into nu-metal, going funky instrumentally and real rap-like on the vocals. Burning Red was even produced by Ross Robinson, sonic mastermind behind the subgenre's giants, Korn and Limp Bizkit.

In an age where Alien Ant Farm hit with a nu-metal cover of Michael Jackson's "Smooth Criminal," Machine Head was right there, too, with their take on "Message in a Bottle" by the Police.

So were they sellouts or—in the vein of Metallica—did Machine Head expertly adapt, adopt, and evolve to survive among the fittest?

Well, they're still at it. Multiple albums, record companies, internecine wars, style changes, and the resurgence of real metal later, Machine Head remains one of the top heavy acts on earth.

After dropping *The Blackening* in 2007, a brutal return to form and a leap forward at the same time, Machine Head opened for Metallica throughout the world on the Death Magnetic tour, and then joined Slayer and Megadeth for a trek through Canada.

Unto the Locust, produced by Machine Head front man Robb Flynn and recorded at Green Day's favorite studio, proved in late 2011 that this was a band for all ages—and stages—of metal magnitude. All the parts work, all the time. Hard.

MARILYN MANSON

Glamour ghoul Marilyn Manson would pertain to Metallica if only as the end-of-the-millennium avatar of Alice Cooper, hard rock's top-selling guillotine-edged pop-cult androgynoid out there peddling death and perversion like candy and nuts to a nation of adolescent nihilists too adolescent to spell "nihilism," let alone to know how to do it right.

Assessment of the differing qualities in the approaches and (ah, yes!) music of Alice and Marilyn remains subjective (and you do have to pick a side, so pick one), but the Manson-Metallica connection runs interestingly deep in that former MM bassist Jeordie White (aka Twiggy Ramirez) nearly replaced outgoing four-stringer Jason Newsted.

White appears in the documentary *Some Kind of Monster* (2002) as the chief competitor of Corrosion of Conformity's Pepper Keenan and Suicidal Tendencies' Robert Trujillo to occupy Metallica's voided bass slot. Trujillo, of course, got the gig, but it's intriguing to ponder how close White got, given the heavy groove and often dance-oriented pump of Marilyn Manson's signature rhythms.

Another Manson-Metallica parallel is that of real-life, media-sensationalized teenage crime.

In 1999, Marilyn Manson found himself in the national crosshairs following the Columbine High School massacre, during which a pair of outcast students gunned down their classmates before eating their own bullets.

The shooters shared a penchant for gothic techno music, which may or may not have included Marilyn Manson. Regardless, in popular culture, Manson took the brunt of the blame, and he rushed to numerous media outlets to defend both himself and extreme music—sometimes eloquently, sometimes obnoxiously, always generating free publicity.

Metallica protested not their own innocence, but that of a trio of convicted killers known as the West Memphis Three. Their story is detailed in the documentary *Paradise Lost: The Child Murders at Robin Hood Hills* (1996) and its sequels *Paradise Lost 2: Revelations* (2000) and *Paradise Lost 3: Purgatory* (2011).

At the heart of the West Memphis Three controversy was the murder and mutilation of three eight-year-old boys in Arkansas. Three teens went to prison for this atrocity, claiming that they were suspected, arrested, and convicted based more on their love of heavy metal music and culture than on any actual evidence. In

2011, the West Memphis Three were freed after serving seventeen years.

Numerous metal and hard rock musicians had rallied (ultimately, with success) to reopen the investigation. Earliest and foremost among these was Metallica, who allowed their music to be used in the *Paradise Lost* films—the first time the band approved that for any movie.

For most, the inner torments of growing up are eased by the discovery of hard rock that expresses those torments outwardly. And then there are others for whom, maybe, just listening or banging their own heads or (best of all) starting their own bands is not enough. Metallica and Marilyn Manson have each been pulled in when those lines blur; the arc between their styles runs dark and deep.

Maybe that explains Lars and Kirk publicly smooching in eyeliner around the time Marilyn released *Antichrist Superstar*. Or maybe not.

MINISTRY

Chicago label Wax Trax pumped death disco into the veins of hard rock throughout the 1980s. Head pusherman in charge was dreadlocked narco-/necro-fetishist Al Jourgensen, and the headiest buzz came by way of his main dope of choice, Ministry.

Jourgensen now mocks Ministry records from the first half of the '80s as wussy synth-pop, and he's not wrong. But upon the release of *The Land of Rape and Honey* in 1987, he and the band had clearly (and loudly) imbibed the migraine monstrosities of industrial pioneers Throbbing Gristle and contemporary New York noisemongers Swans, and then effectively puked them back out over the dance sounds.

The Mind Is a Terrible Thing to Taste, two years later, rocked even harder and mudballed them with perfect-storm velocity toward the watershed vortex of 1991.

The period wherein Metallica's Black Album debuted at #1 may have been the only time for Ministry to score a bona fide MTV hit, and that's just what happened with "Jesus Built My Hot

Rod," a neuron-frying race-crash rave-up that features on lead vocals Gibby Haynes of the Butthole Surfers (who were still a half-
decade away from having their own pop chart bum rush).

The accompanying album, *Psalm 69*, established Ministry not
only as a metal band, but one of the biggest metal bands in the world.

Glue-sniffing mop-swingers in *Kill 'Em All* shirts found they
could identify with Ministry's supersonic sensory-overdrive orgias-
tic excess, while the pleather-encased decadents of the dominatrix
and/or designer drug trades upped their rush factor by way of
Metallica's drop-tuned, Marshall-stacked arena-rumbling hyper-
amplification.

Thus, again, metal pushed forward.

Party till you puke till you choke on it till you're dead. And then
the real fun starts.

PRIMUS

Among their copious other p(l)op-cultural achievements, Bay Area
freak-funk chord benders Primus created and perform the theme
song to *South Park*.

Metallica's James Hetfield sings "Hell Isn't Good" from *South
Park: Bigger, Longer, and Uncut* (1999).

Coincidence?

Oh, yes.

But that doesn't mean Primus and Metallica don't go way back
and haven't shared all kinds of fun times and frightmares together.

For one, following Cliff Burton's death in 1986, visionary bassist Les Claypool auditioned to replace him in Metallica. He didn't
get the gig, but his rejection (in favor of Jason Newsted) prompted
Claypool to profoundly muscle up on behalf of his own semi-flail-
ing outfit, Primus.

Claypool and a rotating guitar-and-drums lineup had been gigging for the previous two years. He became freshly determined to
take Primus to heights previously unimaginable for a power trio
trafficking in dirty-mouthed, string-popping, jazz-/Zappa-/Dr.
Demento–influenced avant-metal.

It certainly worked out.

After turning down the opportunity to join Exodus, Claypool rocketed Primus to cult stardom on par with that of contemporaneous hippie weirdies Phish while also releasing several albums that rank among the most bizarre mainstream hits (1992's *Sailing the Seas of Cheese* and 1993's *Pork Soda*, in particular) and scoring a popular MTV oddity, "Wynona's Big Brown Beaver." In 1993, Primus headlined Lollapalooza, beating Metallica by three years.

The banjo you hear on Metallica's 1998 cover of "Tuesday's Gone" by Lynyrd Skynyrd is being played by Les Claypool, while the distinct guitar driving "Electric Electric" on the 1999 Primus album *Antipop* is being played by James Hetfield.

Primus and Metallica are two practitioners of the very best in bad taste that prove, time and again, to taste great together.

RAGE AGAINST THE MACHINE

Further to the communist left (they said) than the MC5 while raking in more righteous corporate bucks than the MC5 times (MC)5 million, Rage Against the Machine built an explosively efficacious vehicle to deliver their massively capital-generating anticapitalist message.

Piloting this sonic Soviet tank, Tom Morello invented the definitive '90s alt-metal guitar attack—massive pitch-black blasts launched skyward as serrated cannon fire. Chant-happy Zack de la Rocha provided flamethrower vocals.

As much as their philosophy mirrored *Maximum Rocknroll*–type hardcore punk, Rage (to its credit) proudly identified and performed as a heavy metal concern—adding hip-hop notes to the agitprop of crusties like Discharge and Crass and the volume of antiwar thrashers like Sepultura and Nuclear Assault to the pop charts and MTV, selling Marxism by the sound (more than 16 million units shifted to date, comrade).

After their triumphant *The Battle of Los Angeles* in 1999, Rage took a play from Metallica and issued *Renegades*, a table-of-influences covers album, in which they played songs by Minor Threat, the Stones, the Stooges, Cypress Hill, and, yes, the MC5. Here's hoping everybody got paid.

RAMMSTEIN

Rammstein is what would have happened if somebody spiked the barrels at a vintage Munich Beer Hall Putsch with ecstasy.

Half a dozen fire-breathing sadomasochistic Berliners, spray-coated in rubber, leather, and all infectious fluid agents both known and unknown, violate every tenet of the Geneva Convention with guitars, synths, preprogrammed oil-drum percussion, and Kraut chants.

The music is huge, driving, and destructive, like a motorcycle made of chain saws revving up in vat of black blood. You can dance and/or sodomize corpses to it.

Live, Rammstein shows incorporate flamethrowers and onstage sex acts (that also happen to involve flamethrowers).

The 2009 video for the song "Pussy" showcases the members of the band pubes-deep in a variety of porn actresses' organs for which the song is named.

Rammstein's official motto is: "Do your own thing—and then overdo it!"

In case anybody couldn't tell.

As part of the Neue Deutsche Härte ("New German Hardness") movement, which Die Krupps (who have performed numerous industrial tributes to Metallica) are also a part of, Rammstein might have remained popular only among marginal fetishists.

Wider recognition came via their continually influential self-titled single "Rammstein" (sort of like their version of "Hey, Hey, We're the Monkees!") on the soundtrack to David Lynch's *Lost Highway* (1997), and their rubbing black whalebone corsets with Marilyn Manson atop the Walkman playlists of 1999's "Trench-coat Mafia" shooters at the Columbine High School massacre.

Leave it to jackbooted Germans to prove (again) that there's no such thing as bad publicity. The Sex Pistols may have claimed that "Belsen was a gas," but Rammstein makes it sound like a real riot.

RED HOT CHILI PEPPERS

Weezer, the Metallica of guys in high school who fear guys who love

Metallica, brings up two names when asked whose career strategies they most admire and seek to emulate. One is Cliff Burton favorite U2, and the other is the Red Hot Chili Peppers, who, were he still bombing the bass among us, would no doubt also be beloved by Cliff (it is impossible not to picture him waxing Jaco Pastorius for days on end with Flea).

Weezer's reasoning is that U2 and the Peppers, the two biggest mainstream rock acts of the past twenty years, have rung up that success with a signature "alternative" sound that they have broadened and deepened, adapting consistently while maintaining their own terms.

Metallica, who stands shoulder to shoulder with these giants, albeit on the hardest end of the spectrum, can't make the same claim (talk to James about Kirk and Lars's guyliner experiments). This makes the Metallica-Peppers pipeline pump even harder.

Funky punks hanging ten on the crash of first-wave L.A. hardcore, the Red Hot Chili Peppers banged out a series of fairly weird but increasingly successful albums en route to their big-league breakthrough, *Blood Sugar Sex Magik*—one of the Big Slabs on Campus among the rock class of 1991 that also included Metallica's Black Album.

BSSM solidified the superpowered Peppers lineup of peripatetic lip-flapper Anthony Kiedis, parenthetically aforementioned bass dervish Flea, moody string bender John Frusciante, and bull moose Chad Smith slamming skins.

Their hits flew fiery and furious throughout the decade, and where Metallica mis-stepped, the Peppers dug in deeper, releasing their confessional post-addiction magnum opus *Californication* in 1998. Mature, powerful, and universally acclaimed, this was the album *St. Anger* might have been had saner heads (i.e., anyone else's) prevailed.

By *Stadium Arcadium* in 2005, the Chili Peppers simply ruled as rock royalty. Metallica, adrift in post-*Anger* Armageddon, followed them on the path toward the light.

The first step was hiring longtime Peppers producer Rick Rubin to helm their next album, 2008's *Death Magnetic*. The second was graciously accepting Flea's induction of them into the Rock and Roll Hall of Fame in 2009.

Throwing horns as he took the stage, Flea said in his speech, which you can watch on YouTube: "In 1984, I was on tour with my band, in the middle of America somewhere—it was three or four o'clock in the morning—we were all crammed into our van.

It was raining outside, [we were] tired, [had] been on the road, and this music comes on the radio.

And I couldn't believe that it fucking existed.

It was like I had been living in this normal world, where I knew what everything was that came on the radio, and all of a sudden my mind was being blown, by this beautiful, violent thing that was unlike anything I had ever heard before in my life. METALLICA!"

Flea said it all.

ROB ZOMBIE

White Zombie began its undead life as ugly '80s downtown New York City sewer-pipe-bangers, a skunky dropout cabal clanging up gunky rackets on the topics of grind-house horrors, rat guts, and diseases unique to dirty punks.

To say that early White Zombie efforts such as *Psycho-Head Blowout* (1987) and *Make Them Die Slowly* (1989) "stink" is not to disparage them—it's to accurately describe what the music smells like. And it's a compliment.

Steadily, leader Rob Zombie and bassist/ex-girlfriend/curl-swirling dervish Sean Yseult scrubbed away the grime and upped an odd danceability factor. Following the world-turned-upside-down hard rock onslaught of 1991, White Zombie signed to Geffen Records. Then, following Beavis & Butt-Head going berserk for the "Thunderkiss 65" video in 1993, White Zombie became heavy metal superstars.

The band scored another pop hit with the flung-into-the-future sound of "More Human Than Human" in '96. A year later, when Rob oversaw the soundtrack to Howard Stern's *Private Parts* movie and performed the theme song "American Nightmare" as a solo artist, the band broke up. Unfortunately for them, the public barely seemed to notice. Fortunately for metal fans, Rob Zombie immediately took flight as one of the medium's great Renaissance madmen.

Rob Zombie's ascendance mirrors Metallica's in that as he sold more records, the true essence of his innermost artistic sensibilities only grew stronger. Zombie's visual aesthetic, awash in monster movies, hot rods, comic books, tattoos, pulp sci-fi, vintage pinups, and Halloween drag translates seamlessly into his groove-intensive, electro-growl throw-downs and bust-ups. In destroying what he started out as, Rob Zombie became what he was truly meant to be.

More Zombie-like still, Rob transcended mere music as a heavy metal medium to become one of the most controversial horror filmmakers of all time. His remakes *Halloween* (2007) and *Halloween II* (2009) divide fans, but his original visions—*House of 1000 Corpses* (2003), *The Devil's Rejects* (2005), and *The Haunted World of El Superbeasto* (2009) are just that: originals.

And so is their creator.

SOUNDGARDEN

Soundgarden opened for Metallica on the 1996 Lollapalooza tour, a seeming slab of Seattle grunge authenticity opposite headliners so "anti-alternative" that festival founder Perry Farrell quit the entire operation in protest.

Grunge, of course, has its deepest roots in heavy metal and FM-radio monster rock while running on engines powered by punk.

Did any bands ever think of that before the first time the whole world heard "Smells Like Teen Spirit?"

Ah, yes . . . Metallica.

So the truth is that, yes, the bazillion-selling macho marauders of mid-'90s Metallica may have been an odd fit for Lollapalooza's corporate spin on underground prettiness (and pettiness), but not entirely.

And, for sure, Metallica and Soundgarden had long been meant to play together. For without Metallica's initial fusion of metal and punk, there might have been no grunge. And without Soundgarden, there might have been no "Enter Sandman."

For real.

Kirk Hammett said so in 2008.

When explaining the genesis of the "Sandman" opening, Hammett revealed to *Rolling Stone*: "Soundgarden had just put out *Louder Than Love*. I was trying to capture their attitude toward big, heavy riffs. It was two o'clock in the morning. I put it on tape and didn't think about it. When Lars heard the riff, he said, 'That's really great. But repeat the first part four times.' It was that suggestion that made it even more hooky."

Soundgarden hit Seattle in 1984, fronted by superhumanly charismatic singer Chris Cornell and brooding guitar guru Kim Thayil. Local DJ and future Sub Pop Records cofounder Jonathan Poneman immediately deemed them "everything a rock band should be."

In 1986, Soundgarden contributed songs (along with the Melvins and Green River, who later split into Mudhoney and Pearl Jam) to the moment-defining *Deep Six* compilation—this was the grunge equivalent of Metallica, Ratt, and Malice appearing on the 1982 *Metal Massacre* cassette.

Rocketing through Seattle's punk scene, Soundgarden flouted hardcore conventions by going all beardy-longhair, playing long and slow, and eagerly inviting comparisons to standby safety-pin-set whipping boys on the order of Neil Young and Led Zeppelin. Again, one does not need to leap far to see the parallels here with Metallica, clad in Exploited T-shirts, introducing headbangers to Killing Joke.

After releasing increasingly popular records on SST and Sub Pop, Soundgarden became the first of Seattle's grungies to sign with a major, delivering *Badmotorfinger* for A&M in 1991 (shortly thereafter, their neighbors Nirvana made a deal with David Geffen, while at the same time, Kirk Hammett was perfecting that aforementioned riff in preparation for the Black Album).

Not punk anymore, not entirely metal, but as hard and heavy as anybody, Soundgarden toured with Skid Row and Guns N' Roses. Following a 1992 Lollapalooza slot, Soundgarden then found itself to simply be, shock of shocks, a huge mainstream rock band.

And they only got huger.

Superunknown debuted at #1 on the *Billboard* chart in 1994, pumping out one instant radio staple after another: "Black Hole Sun," "Spoonman," "Fell on Black Days," and "My Wave" among them.

In the meantime, Metallica mushroomed into the single biggest hard rock band in the history of the world.

So for these two powerhouses to share a stage in 1996 could only make perfect sense.

It's a long way to the top if you want to rock 'n' roll. And if you get really lucky, you can royally annoy Perry Ferrell into an "I quit!" hissy fit once you get there.

SYSTEM OF A DOWN

The most daring and imaginative of the New Metallicas in turn-of-the-millennium Metallicaland, System of a Down actually changed their name from "Victims of a Down" at least in part so they'd be filed in record stores near their idols, Slayer.

No matter. With their intricacies, eccentricities, spine-snapping agility, and inherent aptitude to speak to and for an audience that had unknowingly been waiting for them to happen, System of a Down is very directly of the Metallica mold. But then, at the same time, SOAD are very much their own mold makers—and, repeatedly, breakers.

System's four Armenian-American upstarts—Serj Tankian (lead vocals, keyboards, rhythm guitar), Daron Malakiain (guitar, vocals), Shavo Odadjian (bass, background vocals), and John Dolmayan (drums)—built up to speed at the dawn of Internet file sharing.

Prior to the one-touch, instant-Lars-nervous-breakdown concept of Napster, mid-'90s metal fans e-mailed each other MP3s of SOAD's three-song demo—very much (ironically enough) in the manner that Metallica's pre-contract *No Life 'Til Leather* cassette established their cult following among tape traders before the band even had a record deal.

As a result, SOAD made a meaningful impact with their first release, 1998's self-titled *System of a Down*. They earned a dream tour slot opening for Slayer at Ozzfest and, show by show, surged toward their mega-platinum breakthrough in 2001, *Toxicity*.

"Chop Suey," the album's wacko hit single, ranks among the weirdest things to ever storm pop radio—a Zappa-esque, stop-start-and-stomp angular freak-out punctuated by screamed chants, driving acoustics, graceful slowdowns, and chaotic napalm blasts that culminate with the verbatim pleas of Christ dying on the cross.

The song had already captivated and catapulted the young hard rock audience aching for more than nu-metal was providing and then, after the September 11 World Trade Center attacks, the serrated madness of "Chop Suey" often sounded like the only music that made any sense.

September 11 played even more seriously into System of a Down's evolution, as vocalist Tankian almost immediately publicly spoke out against U.S. imperialism. Even after a quick flash of criticism, the singer and his bandmates stood their ground, declaring their commitment to peace and frequently invoking the 1915 Armenian Genocide that decimated their ancestors. Eventually, Tankian and Rage Against the Machine guitarist formed the "anti-racist, anti-fascist" activist organization Axis of Justice.

Metallica, at the same time, was suing its own fans who downloaded old music from Napster.

SOAD's commitment to personal vision and integrity (to the point of guitarist Daron Malakian screaming "FUUUUUUUCK!" on *Saturday Night Live* in 2005) only boosted their worth among listeners—three of the band's five albums debuted at #1 on the *Billboard* chart—but none of that would matter if their music didn't remain at once challenging and accessible, befuddling and inspiring.

Metallica would find their way back to that place by the end of the 2000s, and System of a Down served as one of their most respectful and respectable guides.

TOOL

Maynard James Keenan is dark. And deep. And cold.

Keenan's band, Tool, is even darker . . . and deeper . . . and colder than the front man himself.

Which is saying something.

Summing up Tool's overall arsenal and methodology in employing it, critic Stephen Thomas Erlewine writes: "Although Metallica wrote their multi-sectioned, layered songs as if they were composers, they kept their musical attack ferociously at street level. Tool didn't. They embraced the artsy, bohemian preoccupations of Jane's Addiction while they simultaneously paid musical homage to the relentlessly bleak visions of grindcore, death metal, and thrash. Even with their post-punk influences, they executed their music with the aesthetic of prog rock, alternating between long, detailed instrumental interludes and lyrical rants in their songs."

No band more effectively barreled through the crack Metallica's 1991 Black Album made for extreme music than Tool, and no band came from farther afield to claim such a unique and permanent place for itself among the Mount Rushmore of alternative metal.

In 1993, MTV boosted Tool by heavily rotating the video for "Sober," a dank, disgusting, but undeniably cool animated short wherein a bone-faced clay homunculus occupies a slummy world of hurt where raw roast beef runs through toilet pipes and you can only hope your face melts off. The clip gave the band a visual signature, made art-world stars of animators the Brothers Quay, and helped Tool's *Undertow* go platinum.

For the rest of the '90s, as Metallica graduated to stadium regality, Tool staggered out with a succession of stark moans and wails from the underground that plunged the band further and further into the mainstream.

Are they rock stars? That doesn't feel like it fits, but Tool has acquired a hard-core cult following of millions upon millions of devotees worldwide. Their music has won over an array of audiences from Pink Floyd fans aiming to travel into whatever blackness awaits way beyond the dark side of the moon, to thoughtful thrash kids who couldn't stomach the wussiness of New Wave but also couldn't shake the feeling of recognition they got from its more fatalistic practitioners, to an entire generation to whom Metallica is merely the gateway to everything hard rock.

In 1999, Keenan fronted legendary guitar technician Billy

Howerdel's rotating-member supergroup A Perfect Circle, whose notable other players have included Smashing Pumpkins guitarist James Iha and Marilyn Manson bassist Jeordie White (who nearly replaced Jason Newsted in Metallica).

Remarkably, A Perfect Circle came to rival Tool as one of the mainstream rock's most inspired and provocative outfits throughout the past two decades. Both groups remain active and continually evolving.

On top of all this, Tool came up with the song title "Stinkfist." If they had only done that, you'd likely be reading about them in any heavy metal book written by me. Fortunately, they have done, and continue to do, so much more.

1991: THE YEAR *METALLICA* (BY METALLICA) BROKE

These years happen—in culture, in politics, and, for sure, in music—where suddenly what just seemed like another twelve months shapes up to be a before-and-after line.

As pertains to Metallica, there are a series of such years. Punk slammed the world in 1977; the New Wave of British Heavy Metal crested in 1979; and 1986 was the ultimate thrash bash, as a result of Metallica's *Master of Puppets*, Slayer's *Reign in Blood,* and Megadeth's *Peace Sells . . . but Who's Buying?* (Anthrax sandwiched the moment with *Spreading the Disease* in '85 and *Among the Living* in '87).

Still, those sea changes were all focused on single genres. In 1991, the whole of rock (especially hard rock) was upended, with punk, metal, thrash, and all their variants colliding together to revolutionize the mainstream.

Above all, two records drove this watershed moment: *Nevermind* by Nirvana and *Metallica* by Metallica, which is more commonly known as the Black Album.

Aside from local scenes and isolated forms simply bubbling up to the surface as they reflected the cynical energy and post-'80s antagonism of Generation X, a radical, newly accurate approach to tracking music sales changed everything.

In 1991, *Billboard* magazine incorporated the use of SoundScan, a computerized device on record store cash registers that reported exactly what titles and artists had been purchased. In all the decades prior, *Billboard* simply used to call stores and ask whoever picked up the phone what was selling. Their charts were based on that remarkably unscientific and easily corruptible information.

SoundScan provided indisputable facts. Metallica and Nirvana were immediate beneficiaries but so, too, were we all, as rock radio expanded to play new artists and MTV put videos previously perceived as too risky into heavy rotation.

It just so happened that 1991 brought with it, as well, an astonishing array of paradigm-shattering works by a vast spectrum of hard rock outfits at the outset and/or the pinnacle of their games.

Anthrax—*Attack of the Killer B's*
Babes in Toyland—*To Mother*
Cannibal Corpse—*Butchered at Birth*
Dinosaur Jr.—*Green Mind*
Down—underground demos
Guns N' Roses—*Use Your Illusion 1* and *2*
Kyuss—*Wretch*
L7—*Smell the Magic*
Melvins—*Bullhead* and *Lysol*
Metallica—*Metallica*
Monster Magnet—*Spine of God*
Morbid Angel—*Blessed Are the Sick*
Motörhead—*1916*
Mudhoney—*Every Good Boy Deserves Fudge*
My Bloody Valentine—*Loveless*
Nirvana—*Nevermind*
Pearl Jam—*Ten*
Primus—*Sailing the Seas of Cheese*
Prong—*Prove You Wrong*

Red Hot Chili Peppers—*Blood Sugar Sex Magik*
Sepultura—*Arise*
Skid Row—*Slave to the Grind*
Smashing Pumpkins—*Gish*
Soundgarden—*Badmotorfinger*
TAD—*8-Way Santa*
U2—*Achtung Baby*
Urge Overkill—*The Supersonic Storybook*

7

(ANESTHESIA) PULLING TEETH: DOOM METAL AND STONER ROCK

As you've read so far in this book more times than I care to count (but don't let that stop you), it begins with Black Sabbath.

Doom metal first bloomed from the rain sound that opens Black Sabbath's debut. Rock's fate was secured, the heavens rumbled, and Tony Iommi sealed the tomb with the devil's triton. Perdition and the void. Heavy and metal. Then and forever.

Stoner rock billowed biliously to life a year later, upon the hacking cough that first lights up Sabbath's "Sweet Leaf." Weed and electrified instruments had, of course, been making beautiful music for some time by then, but when Ozzy lyrically thanked marijuana for introducing him to his own mind, "Sweet Leaf" introduced several subsequent generations of metal and punk musicians to a very specific pot-powered potential of mixing reefer and riffs.

Doom metal, which took hold in '70s, and stoner rock, which in its present form sprang from the desert storms of Kyuss in the '90s, have always made perfect bong-fellows.

And what thrash was to the mid-'80s, doom and stoner bands are to the hard rock of today.

Metallica has drawn from many of the original doom giants (Candlemass, Trouble, Witchfinder General) and has played with a number of modern stoner acts (High on Fire, Mastodon, the Sword).

Tune in, turn on, bang head.

BLOOD FARMERS

They're named after the 1972 B movie *Invasion of the Blood Farmers*, which I always refused to rent as a teenager because it was only rated PG.

Fortunately, the music of the Blood Farmers is strictly unrated in the *Dawn of the Dead* and Joe Spinell's *Maniac* sense, which is fitting, as guitarist Dave Depraved (aka David Szulkin) labors tirelessly for extreme horror distributors Grindhouse Releasing and wrote the single greatest book ever dedicated to one movie, the self-explanatory *Last House on the Left*.

Blood Farmers formed in 1989, put out their self-titled underground classic in '95, then split up until 2007, when at last the world caught up to the gore-slopped sludge-fuzz these hellhounds pioneered. Do not miss them live. Pressure them to record anew!

THE DEVIL'S BLOOD

The Jefferson Airplane of doom, the Devil's Blood hails from the Netherlands, in both a literal and an eternal-damnation sense. The singer, an unholy twin-peaked mountain incarnating the scorn for which hell hath no fury like, boasts a physical voluptuousness that is dwarfed, divinely, by the inferno columns of her vocal firepower.

Her brother is the guitarist and main songwriter. They and the rest of the prying Dutchmen in the Devil's Blood originally never disclosed their given (or, worse, "Christian") names, and perform sopped in hot red plasma. Presumably, it's the fluid of their name and, more importantly, their sound.

They rhapsodize over black magic and Roky Erickson's "White Faces," of "Christ or Cocaine" (is it really a choice?), of "Feeding the Fire with Tears and Blood," and, in "I'll Be Your Ghost," of romance in a manner that even the most moribund Metallica fan could include on a Valentine's Day mix tape, as it involves a bed of nails and a whipping post.

Love springs infernal.

ELECTRIC WIZARD

From Dorset, UK, comes the oft-proclaimed "heaviest band in the universe." Electric Wizard unquestionably looks the part—bearded warlocks led fronted by Jus Osborn and studded by ice-witch Liz

Buckingham on rhythm axe—and they sound it even more than they look it.

For its first five years, Electric Wizard put forth effective-enough variations on the Black Sabbath formula; they genuinely cracked the cosmos open in 2000 with the rules-of-(dis)engagement-changing *Dopethrone*.

Backstage tumult split EW up seemingly a billion times over the course of the next decade, and yet it proved just the proper alchemical element for the band to concoct at least two more classics, *Witchcult Today* (2007) and *Black Masses* (2010).

HIGH ON FIRE

Arguments can (and will) be made, convincingly, that High on Fire will forever rage in the shadow of its ancestor group, Sleep, and its two mighty stoner milestones: *Sleep's Holy Mountain* in 1993 and 60-minute, single-song marijuanoid magnum opus *Jerusalem*, which, after nearly a decade of fumbles and stumbles, finally received official release as *Dopesmoker* in 2003.

Sleep was a great band and those remain great, indispensible albums, but guitarist Matt Pike's High on Fire is his presently active outfit, and every one of their records so far has been worthy of sparking one up over.

In keeping with their name, High on Fire is faster, hotter, and more infernal than Sleep. The lyrics incorporate reliable metal fantasy elements (Vikings, horses made of flames, "Blessed Black Wings"), yet dodge corniness by sheer force of awesome.

THE HOOKERS

Another unfortunate example of how being ahead of one's time is essentially a curse, the doomy-stony fat-slab Sab-boogie of Lexington, Kentucky's Hookers arrived ten years too early to crest atop a black-blooded wave that they in no small part got rolling.

Hatched from the sort of southern death punk typified by Antiseen, the Hookers added a bit more Slayer and a load more Samhain into a heady beheading balm on the albums *Satan's Highway*, *Black Visions of Crimson Wisdom*, and *Horror Rises from the Tomb*.

KYUSS

Kyuss would be revered as the Metallica of twenty-first century stoner rock if only the band, in its original form, could have lasted long enough to reap the smoking fruits of their heavy '90s labors. Fortunately, everybody else on earth did.

Instead, Kyuss is more often likened to the Velvet Underground of the movement, in that, while their own number of records sold seems small, the influence those records had has been immeasurably huge.

Kyuss wafted skyward in 1990 like the heat itself from the sands of Palm Desert, California. Teenage friends John Garcia (vocals), Josh Homme (guitar), Nick Oliveri (bass), and Brant Bjork (drums) would drive out to remote locales, plug in, and blast their amps out into the endless scorched earth around them.

Their 1992 debut, *Blues for the Red Sun*, as AllMusic.com puts it, "took the underground metal world by storm and established the signature Kyuss sound once and for all: the doom heaviness of Black Sabbath, the feedback fuzz of Blue Cheer, and the space rock of Hawkwind, infused with psychedelic flashes, massive grooves, and a surprising sensibility for punk rock, metal, and thrash."

The recipe for the next two decades of the best hard rock is laid out right there.

Upon breaking up, Kyuss fragmented into a number of nearly-as-vital groups, including Eagles of Death Metal, Mondo Generator, Fu Manchu, and, most significantly, Queens of the Stone Age.

Fronted by Josh Homme on both guitar and vocals, Queens of the Stone Age followed Metallica's Black Album approach to some degree by embracing pop elements, however strained, that exposed the music to an entire new audience—i.e., the rest of the world.

QOTSA scored a massive underground smash in 2000 with "Feel Good Hit of the Summer," a sweepingly cinematic-sounding brain-beater that consists only of a list of intoxicants chanted over an increasingly frenzied heavy metal rave-up.

A year later, the band cracked the big time with one of the decade's great commercial rock hits, "No One Knows."

In 2009, Homme joined Dave Grohl and Led Zeppelin's John Paul Jones as Them Crooked Vultures. Impossibly, it worked.

MASTODON

Atlanta's endlessly ambitious Mastodon personifies metal in our media-fractured modern times.

They are punk, they are prog, they are heavy, and they are heady—and yet they aim for the gonads and under no circumstances does their music go down easy.

Tattoo-faced front man Brent Hinds often bottoms out into death metal vocals while the band behind him goes grindcore.

Leviathan, Mastodon's 2004 breakthrough album, retells the story of Moby-Dick. The 2007 follow-up, *Blood Mountain*, spins the epic yarn of a climbing expedition that includes encounters with supernatural hunters and a plasma-drinking deer-god. Two thousand nine's *Crack the Skye* concerns the time-space wormhole travels of an astral-projecting paraplegic who enters Rasputin's body to battle the devil.

Yet these boys like to drink beer and break shit.

Mastodon tours with old-school no-fun real-dealers like Slayer and Lamb of God, and then they compose the opening song for the *Aqua Teen Hunger Force* movie and perform as part of a live caravan promoting the Cartoon Network.

The band members are legitimately frightening roughneck shit-stirrers, but their audience is often packed with indie hipsters in skinny jeans. The last big-time outfit to take on so many seemingly contradictory components would be no less than Metallica.

And while Mastodon is not likely to ever evolve toward Metallica's mass appeal, their 2011 release *The Hunter*—their first non-concept album in years—debuted at #11 in *Billboard* and sold 41,000 copies in its first week.

That's a shocking figure for any metal band in this free-music Internet age, but especially so for a band that appeals so much to the very demographic that's the very best at downloading whatever they want for free.

Sometimes, as Metallica and now Mastodon have proven, being

all things to all metal fans only makes them want you to do, and to be, more. And they're willing to pay for the privilege.

THE MELVINS

One of the goddamnedest things to ever slither up from who-knows-what depths to the surface of rock 'n' roll, the Melvins rarely get mentioned in the same rooms, let alone the same references, as Metallica, but if you're a fan of the latter, a multitude of reasons abound for you to investigate the fat, freaky, hairy, unhinged other.

First and foremost, the Melvins rock. Lumped often (and not inaccurately) with psych-punk freak farms such as Flipper and the Butthole Surfers, the Melvins have always—even when they started out as a hardcore band playing Cream covers—been a stoner metal outfit.

They specialize in mucky, mucked-up, deep, rumbling, and, above all, heavy.

Guitarist, singer, and possessor of the freakiest silver witch Afro in this or any other dimension, Buzz "King Buzzo" Osborne traverses in gut-churning down-tuned chords, string-massacring solos, and power vocals on par with those of the most revered axe-slingers and front men in all of doomdom. Drummer Dale Crover is fittingly John Bonham–like in the massiveness of his beats.

Although the Melvins' highest-profile association is with Nirvana (Buzz taught Kurt Cobain how to play guitar), they have also worked regularly with members of Metallica favorites Tool and Faith No More.

They share influences with Metallica, as well, including Tony Iommi as the root of their guitar sound and an unabashed love for Kiss. Buzzo speaks often of the brilliance of Ace Frehley's innovative style, and the band's 1994 major-label foray, *Houdini*, contains a cover of the Kiss chestnut "Going Blind."

The Melvins played the second stage on various stops of the 1997 Metallica-headlined Lollapalooza tour but expressed no love (in not so many words) for the main attraction.

It was a sentiment, of course, shared by throngs of old-school fans who cringed over this incarnation of "Alternica."

"Heavy metal is in bad shape right now," Osborne told the Silicon Valley weekly *Metro* at the time. "There's only Aerosmith—and Sepultura is a great band. Heavy metal is aggressive; it's not dumb college rock, like the revenge-of-the-nerds thing that's going on right now. Whenever I see Weezer on TV, I think Slayer should pop up and cut their throats. I think rock needs to be more aggressive right now. Where's Black Flag when we need them?"

SAINT VITUS

While Metallica brought punk to metal in the '80s by way of their sound, L.A. longhairs Saint Vitus did the reverse in a more impractical fashion. They were the sole 100 percent unquestionably heavy metal act signed in 1984 to punk powerhouse SST Records at the height of the label's indie-culture dominance.

And, still, it was the wrong place, wrong time for Saint Vitus—by which I don't mean SST; I mean the entirety of the mid-'80s musical universe.

SV's dense, sludge-plopping Sabbath-spawned hell-trudge could not have been more at odds not only among fans of SST staples Black Flag, Hüsker Dü, and the Minutemen, but the more straight-up metal world as well, which had gone speed-kicked and thrash-happy thanks to Slayer, Exodus, Anthrax, and, above all, Metallica.

Any member of that last pack would be quick to point out the crucial contribution to their own aesthetic made by Euro doomsters such as Candlemass, Cathedral, or Witchfinder General, or stateside by wild cards such as the sporadically alive-and-on-fire Pentagram and Chicago's Christian super-sludge squadron Trouble.

Yet Saint Vitus, too, often gets left out of too many doom summations' unholy hosanna-hurling. Even the Obsessed, the on-and-off (and also wholly awesome) project of Saint Vitus's sometimes front man Scott "Wino" Weinrich, comes up before SV.

Here's how to properly worship Saint Vitus. Start with *Born Too Late* (a title that would only be more unwittingly ironic if it were *Born Too Soon*) from 1986, the year of *Reign in Blood* and *Master of*

Puppets, and let the alternate sub-rosa metal universe embodied there weigh down and pull you under. Then sink into the rest of Saint Vitus catalogue.

Once you're gone, you can't come back. These guys will tell you all about it. Very, very slowly. So you understand.

SLIPKNOT

In a way, Slipknot is the end of extreme metal—until the next, last extremity.

The nine-piece, costume-clad terror junta—more murderers of ears (and the souls attached to them) than players of instruments—debuted in 1999 with a self-titled LP shocker and a living-seizure stage show (punctuated, not infrequently, by G. G. Allin–esque coprophilia) that achieved the very end limits of what was possible in speed, force, and anti-human brutalism.

Their second album, 2001's *Iowa*, is all that and, somehow, more—a masterpiece of nihilism, misanthropy, and bewitching cacophony, hammering down its never-before-possible assault with homicidal, multitiered percussion and tsunamis of noise that incorporate thrash, rap, techno, death metal, grindcore, crust punk, industrial, and, to be sure, Kiss.

So as with Metallica's milestone moments, the feeling after Slipknot was, "Okay, where does metal go now? What's left?"

There's no answering such questions until they answer themselves. But it does place Slipknot among metal's elite guard, and lead screamer Corey Taylor (aka #8, aka the Great Big Mouth, aka the Sickness) knows and salutes the origin of such exclusive status.

"I remember hearing *Master of Puppets* at a friend's house," he told the industry website Artist Direct. "That line at the end of 'Damage Inc.'—'Fuck it all and fucking no regrets'—was the one that every metalhead waited for with bated breath. When it came, you'd jump up and scream along to it. It was amazing. Metallica will always be important to me!"

Metallica and Slipknot have played together on multiple occasions, frequently at massive festival gatherings. Most remarkable was 2004's Download Festival in the UK's Donington Park, where Lars Ulrich's sudden medical emergency enabled Joey Jordison—Slipknot's main percussionist and producer—to man the skins.

"I could not imagine getting into the seat of one of my heroes," Jordison said afterward. "It was one of the best experiences of my life."

Even more in keeping with their idols, Slipknot burned to go beyond just barbaric abandon. Corey Taylor and guitarist Jim Root returned to their original project, the radio-friendly Stone Sour, as an outlet for their more mainstream musical ideas.

Described by MTV as sounding like "a cross between Metallica and Alice in Chains," Stone Sour has run parallel alongside Slipknot, its own moments of lightness and overall accessibility rendering the latter's utter darkness and punishing hopelessness that much more effective (and vice versa).

It's sort of like if Metallica had been able to get their hair cut and record with Bob Rock while still keeping their original fans happy.

Neat trick, Slipknot.

THE SWORD

Speaking in 2008 to RollingStone.com about his favorite up-and-coming band, Lars Ulrich said: "I'm a product of British metal—Iron Maiden, Saxon, Angel Witch—and the Sword sound like the definitive New Wave of British Heavy Metal, which is interesting coming from four guys from Texas.

"They're not really a young Metallica," Lars summed up, "but that's because they're cooler than we were."

One way that the youthful Austin foursome was cooler than early-'80s Metallica is that, at the time when Lars gushed all this, the Sword was opening for the biggest hard rock band in the history of the world—yes, Metallica.

Success, in fact, came relatively quickly to the Sword. Formed by Led Zeppelin fan J. D. Cronise in 2003, the group released two LPs over the next several years—*Age of Winters* (2006) and *Gods of the Earth* (2008)—and landed a song, "Freya," on the Guitar Hero

II video game. Then Lars Ulrich fell in love with them. The rest is rock stardom.

It's important to reflect on Lars's observation of the Sword's "cool" factor, however. From their skinny-jeaned, trucker-hatted, SXSW festival breakthrough onward, the band has been charged with trafficking in the most reviled-ever form of false metal—the NPR/PBR/*Onion AV Club*–compatible "hipster metal."

There's no denying the skill of the players in delivering Sabbath-black and Purple-deep riffage, but there is something disingenuous, maybe even offensively so, in the Sword's retro-metal fantasy tropes.

Guys getting this much poon—and adoration from *The New York Times*, but especially the poon—simply don't have the pissed-off-for-being-so-pissed-upon Dungeons-and-Dragons-dork credibility to pull off a sci-fi rock opera titled *Warp Riders*. Especially not three albums in. Or ever.

Yet, of course, Lars Ulrich is hardly the Sword's sole supporter. The band has recorded with Swedish doom devils Witchcraft and toured with legitimate headbanging ham-fists on the order of Clutch, Machine Head, and Lamb of God—even if the Sword does fit in so much more comfortably with such indie-acceptable acts as Baroness, Isis, and Pelican.

Listen for yourself and decide. Vehemently.

SUICIDE AND REDEMPTION
The Grunge Story

From the Pacific Northwest came a sound fittingly reminiscent of burly lumberjacks, caffeinated mermaids, sweaty flannel, and all variations on Sasquatch. It was punk first, but it was also heavily metal, and it borrowed maybe even more from '70s arena rock. Nobody knows who called it "grunge" first, but that was the name bandied about this sound and, oh, did it stick.

The grunge sound is sludgily down-tuned, fuzzily distorted guitars, wailing vocals, and wildly varying tempos. Side two of Neil Young's *Rust*

Never Sleeps is a good reference point, as is much of the catalogue of grunge's most frequently covered band, Kiss.

Seattle's Sub Pop Records evolved out of a fanzine of the same name and functioned to grunge as Megaforce did to thrash.

During the year that Metallica put forth the Black Album, Sub Pop followed up a promising '89 release, *Bleach*, by a band named Nirvana, with an album called *Nevermind*. You may be familiar with both artist and title.

Perfectly nailed by SiriusXM's Ian Christe as "a Beatles-influenced version of heavy metal screaming full throttle," *Nevermind* is credited or (depending on the speaker) decried as putting metal out to pasture for a spell, or at least forcing it underground.

While Slaughter and White Lion may not have recovered, Nirvana, on the contrary, broadened both metal's fan base and possibilities—especially Metallica's. And their heavy sound was no mistake.

According to Nirvana drummer and world-class headbanger Dave Grohl: "Kurt and [bassist] Krist Novoselic would listen to Celtic Frost and the Smithereens, and that's what they imagined themselves to sound like."

Grunge only made Metallica stronger. Just as they adapted to take their sound worldwide, the world adapted to go Metallica-wide. Look no further than Alice in Chains for the perfect example.

Any one of the following grunge milestones should be explored by the Metallica enthusiast. Except maybe Pearl Jam. They're just on the list because . . . they're Pearl Jam. Like 'em or lump 'em.

7 Year Bitch—*Viva Zapata*
Alice in Chains—*Facelift*, *Dirt*, *Jar of Flies*
Babes in Toyland—*Fontanelle*
Dinosaur Jr.—*You're Living All Over Me*, *Bug*, *Green Mind*
Green River—*Come on Down*, *Dry as a Bone*, *Rehab Doll*
The Melvins—*Houdini*
Mother Love Bone—*Apple*

Mudhoney—*Superfuzz Bigmuff*

Nirvana—*Bleach, Nevermind, In Utero*

Pearl Jam—*Ten*

Screaming Trees—*Buzz Factory, Uncle Anesthesia, Sweet Oblivion*

Skin Yard—*Hallowed Ground*

Soundgarden—*Ultramega OK, Louder Than Love, Badmotorfinger, Superunknown*

Stone Temple Pilots—*Core, Purple, Tiny Music, Shangri-La Dee Da*

TAD—*God's Balls, 8-Way Santa, Inhaler*

8

HERO OF THE DAY:
METALLICA MOVIES

An argument can be made, strongly, that heavy metal is the most cinematic of rock genres. Each of the following titles, which are essential extensions of the Metallica experience, offer ample evidence. Grab some popcorn and throw your horns.

ANVIL: THE STORY OF ANVIL (2008)

A monumental, moving, funny documentary on unsung Canadian headbanging institution Anvil. As teenagers, the group's leaders—singer Steve "Lips" Kudlow and drummer Robb Reiner—vowed to keep rocking forever. In 1982, upon the release of their speed-metal milestone *Metal on Metal*, that seemed like a solid career plan. A quarter century and no hit records later, the now fifty-something boys are still at it—and the movie will make you love them for it. Anvil is a must for metal fans and movie fans, period; for Metallica fans, it provides an alternate-universe take on what James Hetfield and Lars Ulrich (who appears here) might be like had everything stalled after *Kill 'Em All*.

BEAVIS AND BUTT-HEAD DO AMERICA (1996)

Beavis—aka, on occasion, Cornholio—is forever clad in a Metallica tee. Butt-Head, the brainier half of MTV's hilarious dim cartoon duo, perpetually wears an AC/DC shirt. Not sure if there's a message there, but their big-screen adventure is as gut-busting as the TV show, where the boys famously freaked out to "One" and "For Whom the Bell Tolls" (Butt-Head: "Sit your ass down,

Lars, and play the drums like you're supposed to!" Beavis: "Shut up, Butt-Head! Your mom's a slut!").

THE DARWIN AWARDS (2006)

The Darwin Awards is adapted from the website of the same name, which chronicles true stories of dumb, preventable deaths (the idea being that the deceased upgrade humanity's evolutionary progress by removing themselves from it).

One of the most popular entries involves two ganja-zonked heshers who attempted to crash a Metallica concert, but one ended up crashing his van down on top of the other, who had scaled a fence, from a stupidly dizzying height.

In the movie re-creation, Metallica appears as themselves, performing bits of "No Leaf Clover" and "Sad but True" and acting in a goofy little wrap-up bit at the end.

THE DECLINE OF WESTERN CIVILIZATION PART II: THE METAL YEARS (1988)

Documentarian Penelope Spheeris follows up her punk-themed 1981 first installment with a great, insane, uproarious take on Sunset Strip rock at the (literal) height of hair-metal mania.

Metallica had long since split L.A. for the Bay Area by this time, and the movie's lack of Guns N' Roses seems an odd oversight, but it's a classic snapshot of youth gone (embarrassingly) wild.

Chris Holmes of W.A.S.P. is magnetically pathetic drowning himself in vodka while floating in a pool, and Ozzy Osbourne settles, once and forever, that nobody ever actually mis-heard Jimi Hendrix sing "'Scuse me while I kiss this guy!"

DWC2 ends with a moving and impressive appearance by Megadeth. They come off as smart, committed, witty, and uniquely talented—an accomplishment on its own, a miracle in this milieu of Bill-Gazzarri-chanted "O-din! O-din! O-din!"

THE DEVIL'S ADVOCATE (1997)

You will see Lars Ulrich's old lady naked. Full frontal. Mocking Jesus Christ. It's a hell of a (hot) sight. You will also see, in *The*

Devil's Advocate, a rip-snorting good tale of Satan (a perfect use of Al Pacino at the flaming height of his '90s all-systems-over-the-top hyper-mode) and his lawyer (Keanu Reeves, a perfectly stiff foil) taking Manhattan and, from there, the rest of us. The afore-mentioned paramour of Mr. Ulrich (and mother of his son, Dan-ish beauty Connie Nielsen, costars as a mouthwatering minion of Old Scratch. Two hours and ten minutes in, Connie bares all and strikes a cruciform pose as a first step to instigating Armageddon. You'll also see exactly how she brought about the end of Lars's groupie-chasing world, right in the raw heat of that moment.

ENCINO MAN (1992)

Metal has often been likened to the music of cavemen, so it fits that the Metallica cover of Queen's "Stone Cold Crazy" turns up amusingly in this unfrozen-Neanderthal comedy. Brendan Fraser is the prehistoric find; Pauly Shore is his Jewish surfer pal.

GET THRASHED: THE STORY OF THRASH METAL (2006)

Raw and respectful, authoritative and antiauthoritarian, the docu-mentary *Get Thrashed* effectively traces the roots of thrash through vintage video and conversations with the rockers who laid down those roots, including Lars Ulrich, Anthrax's Scott Ian, and Slayer's Tom Araya and Kerry King.

THE GOOD, THE BAD, AND THE UGLY (1966)

At the suggestion of Megaforce Records founder Jonny Z, since 1983 Metallica has taken the stage to the instrumental "The Ecstasy of Gold" by composer Ennio Morricone. It's a galloping anthem as vast as a Mexican desert sky that underscores the climax of director Sergio Leone's spaghetti western masterpiece, *The Good, the Bad, and the Ugly*. It turned out that Jonny Z didn't have to sell the song hard.

"My favorite film of all time has got to be *The Good, the Bad, and the Ugly*," says James Hetfield, "because there are three characters in it that are completely different, and I find a little piece of myself in each one of them."

In the movie, "the Good" is Clint Eastwood as the stoic and heroic Man with No Name. "The Bad" is wholly evil gunfighter Lee Van Cleef. And "the Ugly" is the backstabbing, sadistically wormy thief played by Eli Wallach.

Any excuse to watch *The Good, the Bad, and the Ugly* is a great one, but as a Metallica fan, it's even more fun to guess what elements of the three principals to which James is referring.

Of note is that Metallica paid this inspiration back by covering "The Ecstasy of Gold" on the 2007 tribute album *We All Love Ennio Morricone*.

HESHER (2010)

Joseph Gordon-Levitt stars as the titular teenage dirtbag in *Hesher*, a scraggle-maned Metalli-head who serves as an inspiring antihero to bullied, beaten, and bedraggled high school loser T. J. (Devin Brochu). Hesher moves in to T. J.'s family garage, where he transforms the life of the kid's sad-sack widowed dad (Rainn Wilson) and depressed neighborhood checkout girl Nicole (Natalie Portman). Often, he improves a situation by blowing something up.

Press materials describing the character of Hesher as a "heavy metal Mary Poppins" are not inaccurate and the film is charming—in large part because it gets the heavy metal right. And that's no doubt greatly a result of upon whom Joseph Gordon-Levitt based his performance: original Metallica bassist Cliff Burton.

Metallica so loved the film that they allowed the movie poster to present the title in the shape of their logo and they allowed an astonishing five of their songs to be played on the soundtrack, including Burton's signature piece, "(Anesthesia) Pulling Teeth."

In addition, the band reached out to Gordon-Levitt, who told website MetalUnderground.com: "Metallica dug the movie. It was a real honor and I took a lot of inspiration for this character from the basis of some of their early albums [and] this guy named Cliff Burton, who played on *Master of Puppets* and *Ride the Lightning*. And when the band saw it, they were like, 'You know what?! He reminds us of Cliff,' and we didn't even tell them that's what we were going for. And they let us use their songs and I was actually moved because I grew up headbanging to Metallica."

Hesher will take you right back to that shared experience. Heshin'.

JOHNNY GOT HIS GUN (1971)

Dalton Trumbo's 1938 antiwar novel got its big-screen treatment in the thick of America's Vietnam torment and then languished largely in obscurity for years. It was rarely ever even mentioned and, if it was, usually someone just pointed out how instantly the movie had dated (Donald Sutherland's appearance as a hippie-fied Jesus most often being cited as the culprit).

Regardless, Trumbo's central story is shockingly original and powerful—the Johnny of the title is a World War I soldier missing his arms, legs, face, and any ability to communicate; we follow his inner monologue.

Discovery of the book prompted Metallica to adapt the plot into their landmark epic "One" on . . . *And Justice for All.*

The existence of the movie also goaded the heretofore MTV-averse band into creating its first music video: an amalgam of performance footage and clips from the film. As such, *Johnny Got His Gun* is strongly recommended if you like Metallica, hippie Jesus and all.

LEMMY (2010)

The connection between Metallica and Motörhead—in particular, the latter's iconic front man, Lemmy Kilmister—cannot be overstated.

The members of Metallica almost make it seem like overstatement is possible, though, in the documentary *Lemmy*, wherein they sing hosannas to this high priest of metal mayhem to a repetitive point that might (almost) prompt a response of, "Okay! We get it!"

But then, when Lemmy joins Metallica live onstage for a barnstorming run-through of Motörhead's "Damage Case," we really do get it.

Lemmy really is that cool. Motörhead really is that great. And

Metallica really is that deeply in debt, and in awe, of this madman and his hyper-propulsive punk-metal creation that just keeps continuing to chug triumphantly across the universe.

With enthusiasm that echoes the giddiness they felt upon first dropping a needle onto Motörhead vinyl, all living Metallica members, past and present, sound off to first-time documentarians Greg Olliver and Wes Orshoski on just how large Lemmy looms in their lives.

Kirk Hammett points out that even pre-Hawkwind and pre-Motörhead, Lemmy earns worship simply for being Jimi Hendrix's roadie.

Robert Trujillo gushes over the terrifying territories to which Lemmy pushed the possibilities of bass-banging.

Jason Newsted waxes galactic over Lemmy's first major ensemble, space rockers Hawkwind, a direct precursor to metallic sci-fi power station Voivod (whom Newsted joined after departing Metallica).

James Hetfield enumerates just a few of the many, many ideas and mannerisms he and Metallica "stole" from Motörhead, including the sound, the power, the vocals, and, most amusingly, the first few years of Hetfield's Lemmy-lifted semi–Fu Manchu facial hair.

Lars Ulrich, as he so often does, simply proclaims himself "the number one Motörhead fan in the world."

Other noteworthy names echo Metallica's hallelujah chorus throughout *Lemmy* and each time, the movie presents more alarming, amazing, and indisputable evidence to establish the proclamation that's made most often: "Lemmy is rock 'n' roll."

To be a fan of Metallica is to know that's true. To watch *Lemmy* is to know, further, that rock 'n' roll is king.

MEGAFORCE (1982)

Barry Bostwick lights up a resplendent, sack-hugging spandex jumpsuit as futuristic action hero Ace Hunter in *Megaforce*, a high-camp sci-fi oddity from the director of *Smokey and the Bandit*.

Although a box-office bomb in its day, *Megaforce* has lived on as a cult favorite for its early-'80s energy and garish special effects (it makes a great triple bill with *Krull* and *Flash Gordon*—or even *Flesh Gordon*).

The film is also indispensible in Metallica history as providing Jonny Z with the name for the fledgling record company that would output the band's first releases.

Originally, the label was to be called Vigilante, but Cliff Burton suggested Megaforce based on the movie team's credo "Deeds, Not Words!" and the poster tagline "When the force was with them, no one stood a chance!"

Those two sentiments nicely nailed the stance of up-and-coming Metallica and the burgeoning thrash metal scene they were forging. In addition, at the time, the band (ironically, except perpetually bell-bottomed Cliff) was still very much sporting the spandex.

The force, as we know now, was with them. And no one stood a chance.

METAL: A HEADBANGER'S JOURNEY (2005)

Metal-loving anthropologist Sam Dunn travels the globe for an all-inclusive study of his (and our) favorite music. Dunn is a great interviewer and his subjects warmly open up, providing a highly useful overview in which, naturally, Metallica figures prominently.

METALLICA: SOME KIND OF MONSTER (2004)

One of cinema's most amazing documentaries, *Metallica: Some Kind of Monster* is also one of the ballsiest moves ever made by rock stars. No multimillionaire superstars has ever allowed themselves to be so nakedly exposed as crybabies, backstabbers, petty grudge-holders, and fools—and then have it work out in their favor!

You will want to repeatedly slap and shout, "GROW UP!" at both James and Lars, but by the end, you can only appreciate what they've allowed us to witness.

As Metallica records the (ultimately disastrous) *St. Anger*, we watch these damaged, angry adults run on resentment and unresolved issues until they (and we) can simply stand no more.

Famously, the group brings in a Cosby-sweatered boob to coach them and, infamously, they absolutely destroy Jason Newsted over his unforgivable sin, a decade and a half earlier, of accepting their invitation to replace the deceased Cliff Burton.

Of particular potency is a visit to Torben Ulrich, Lars's elf-in tennis-pro dad, who assures his son that he'll never be in the league of his rock idols and, upon hearing a new track, coldly says, "Delete that!"

The cocky, art-auctioning, model-banging, Napster-suing rock star crumples into a defeated child right on-screen.

And therein lies the power of *Some Kind of Monster*: When the action wraps up with a performance in a penitentiary, we just want Metallica to win again, because they have proven once again that they are us.

MISSION IMPOSSIBLE II (1999)

Metallica contributed "I Disappear" to the soundtrack of the Tom Cruise sequel, directed by Hong Kong action master John Woo. Lars and Kirk Hammett also reworked the theme song, a duty in the original that had fallen on U2. Again, those guys and those guys. Impossible!

OLD SCHOOL (2003)

The twenty-first-century avatar of *Animal House* (1978) that made Vince Vaughn a comedy star and Will Ferrell a comedy legend features "Master of Puppets" on its amusingly eclectic soundtrack (which also contains songs by Snoop Dogg, Simon and Garfunkel, Whitesnake, and Clint Holmes).

Metallica is famously stringent about selecting what films get to use its music, so perhaps they were inspired to contribute by director Todd Phillips's extreme-rock track record: He directed the classic puke-punk documentary *Hated: G. G. Allin and the Murder Junkies* (1994).

That, or they just watched Ferrell singing "Dust in the Wind" during the funeral scene and decided that they had to be a part of anything as hilarious as that.

PARADISE LOST: THE CHILD MURDERS AT ROBIN HOOD HILLS (1996)

Paradise Lost documents a tragic, sickening slaughter of three eight-year-olds and how a trio of black-clad, metal-listening teens went to jail for the crime. The movie so persuasively argues in favor of the teens' innocence that Metallica donated songs on the soundtrack—the first time the band had allowed any movie to use its music. Two sequels and the real-life freeing of the West Memphis Three (as they had come to be known) eventually followed.

SOUTH PARK: BIGGER, LONGER, AND UNCUT (1999)

The Comedy Central cartoon not only hit cinemas, it did so as an instant classic musical, featuring tunes such as "Uncle Fucker" and the Academy Award–nominated "Blame Canada." James Hetfield sings with Satan on "Hell Isn't Good."

A few years later, the TV show naturally (and hilariously) socked it to Metallica over their anti-Napster shenanigans. James, pointedly, did not sing on that episode.

Let's mention here, too, Metallica's very funny appearance on a 2006 episode of *The Simpsons*. After their bus breaks down, they're offered a ride by Springfield's #1 Metallica fan, stoner school bus driver Otto, a character voiced by Harry Shearer—bassist Derek Smalls of Spinal Tap himself!

THIS IS SPINAL TAP (1984)

The movie to which all rock bands must answer to is *Spinal Tap*—no matter if the group is two-bit and trivial or platinum-selling and stadium-packing.

This is especially true for metal bands, of which *Spinal Tap* presents the ultimate cinematic example.

The fights and failures, the breakdowns and bust-ups and, ultimately, the silliness and satisfaction that make all the (endless) troubles worthwhile are perfectly nailed by director Rob Reiner's mock documentary.

The flawless performances by Michael McKean, Harry Shearer, and (especially) Christopher Guest as the titular British metal powerhouse remain unmatched in the annals of screen comedy and actual, straight-faced rock 'n' roll chronicles—including *Metallica: Some Kind of Monster.*

Also, Spinal Tap beat Metallica to an all-black album cover by seven whole years (although theirs was titled *Smell the Glove*)!

THE TOXIC AVENGER (1985)

The signature sewage-spawned superhero of New York schlock studio Troma Entertainment, the Toxic Avenger figures into Metallica's story not just for his namesake film's quite literally head-banging violence and very metal sense of sick humor.

James Hetfield regularly invokes the movie when describing the 1992 onstage pyrotechnic accident that left him scorched and oozing with third-degree burns, pointing out how his bubbling and blistering skin looked like the scene where a nerd transforms into the title monster in *The Toxic Avenger.*

As Beavis and Butt-Head would put it: "Yes! Cool! Heh-heh."

CLIFF 'EM ALL (1987)

September 27, 1986, not only forever changed Metallica, it changed music.

On that pitch-black night, Metallica lost more than a bassist when a bus crash killed Cliff Burton. They lost their guru, their guiding light, their most accomplished musician, their gateway to new and eclectic sounds, and, above all, they lost their dearly cherished friend and brother.

The world, by extension, lost one of its most promising talents on the rise.

Clifford Lee Burton was twenty-four when he died, a tragedy on every count.

There is, however, a perfect means of celebrating the too-short joy of Burton's life, as well as his legacy that lives on in every hard-rock rhythm section to have arisen in his wake: *Cliff 'Em All*, Metallica's 1987 VHS release of camcorder concert footage, home videos, and private photos showcasing Cliff Burton as his most vibrant and vital.

Cliff 'Em All kicks off with sneakily shot songs from Metallica's opening slot on Ozzy Osbourne's 1986 tour, an opportunity to hear Burton wail on "Creeping Death," "Am I Evil?" "Damage Inc.," and, just months after it had hit vinyl, "Master of Puppets."

The next musical go-round is culled from a 1983 show at San Francisco's beyond intimate club, the Stone. Billed as "Cliff's second gig," you can revel here in Cliff's majestic spotlight solo "(Anesthesia) Pulling Teeth" and ultra-rare footage of original axe-meister Dave Mustaine blazing on lead guitar throughout "Whiplash."

Professionally shot video follows of "The Four Horseman," "Fade to Black," and a particularly powerful "Seek and Destroy" at Germany's 1985 Metal Hammer Festival.

The 1986 Roskilde Festival in Denmark includes "Welcome Home (Sanitarium)" and gloriously extended Cliff solos, followed by "For Whom the Bell Tolls" in Oakland.

Cliff 'Em All's closing numbers are culled from the Chicago stop on Metallica's "Kill 'Em All for One" tour—"No Remorse" and "Metal Militia."

Punctuating the performances are snatches of home videos, previously unseen TV interviews, private pictures, and general clowning.

The sound quality throughout often stinks and much of the video is a shaky-cam-hater's stomach-turning worst nightmare. But *Cliff 'Em All* is raw and it's real and it rocks, very much in the spirit of the parting shot of Cliff Burton offering us a flower with one hand and giving us the finger with the other.

It's that living spirit of Cliff Burton that pulsates on through Metallica. And the rest of us.

ROCK STAR: SUPERNOVA

In 2005, Australian alt-rock didgeridoodlers INXS launched a (successful) search for a new lead singer via the summertime CBS game show *Rock Star*.

The following July, the program returned as *Rock Star: Supernova*, and instead of an existing '80s nostalgia act, vocalists competed to front a prefabricated roster of heavy metal heroes (with varying degrees of actual heroics).

The cheese factor was immediate and, for the most part, to be expected.

First, *RSS* was hosted by Dave Navarro of Jane's Addiction and, more recently, *'Til Death Do Us Part*, MTV's "assisted reality" show documenting his wedding to breast implant model Carmen Electra. Dave of the Cosmos is by no means an enemy of the cheesy.

Drumming for *RSS*: sex-tape tsunami Tommy Lee. Wherever there's cheese, Mötley Crüe's skin-slapper will show up with meat, and plenty of it.

On guitar, we had Gilby Clarke, Izzy Stradlin's replacement in Guns N' Roses, and cultivator of Three Musketeers facial hair that just screams, "*Frommage!*"

And then there was the bassist. Sitting in as a judge on this swelter-weather replacement TV contest—smiling and jiving and keeping a straight face regarding the fashion decisions of Dave Navarro—was Jason Newsted, late of Metallica.

He might have cut his hair a decade earlier, but it was tough to associate "Jason Newkid," of all the band members, with anything this cheeseball.

And, yet, there he was. And there the show was. And, truth be told, *Rock Star Supernova* was a tremendously entertaining excuse to pump the AC and boob-tube it up on Tuesday nights all summer long—and, as a Metallica fan, it never ceased to be fascinating to watch and think, "Jesus frig! That's Jason Newsted involved in this nonsense!"

The band itself was horrific: a cluelessly contrived attempt at a (joyless, songless) Monkees for the Hot Topic generation featuring men who'd sprouted gray pubes years before the first Hot Topic even opened.

But the singers were good, the challenges remained consistently interesting, and some real standout talents emerged, including Portland siren Storm Large, Icelandic baldo Magni Ásgeirsson, freaky South African songbird Dilana Robichaux, and the ultimate winner, simian Canuck (and future husband of porn star Kendra Jade) Lukas Rossi.

The *Rock Star Supernova* album is worth a few YouTube clicks, and Jason Newsted is to be saluted for ditching the live-show tour as soon as a sudden shoulder injury became the remotest bit credible.

Suicidal Tendencies, 1987. (Photofest)

9

DISPOSABLE HEROES:
ROOTS, BRANCHES, AND SIDE PROJECTS

The earliest incarnations of Metallica were known as Phantom Lord and Leather Charm. Grinder, Blitzer, and (most goofily) Red Vette also figured as potential names. Finally, when San Francisco fanzine publisher Ron Quintana ran a list past Lars Ulrich of potential titles for his new publication, "Metallica" leapt out at the drummer. That's why he recommended that Quintana go instead with *Metal Mayhem* and, alas, that became the journal of record for thrash at ground zero.

Although Lars and James Hetfield have been Metallica's only two constant members, there are fewer underpinnings and offshoots than in many other uppermost echelon rock squads.

Most notably, Dave Mustaine created Megadeth as a vehicle of vengeance after Metallica gave him the boot, and his replacement, Kirk Hammett, was pilfered from Exodus.

Following Cliff Burton's 1986 demise, Jason Newsted jumped ship from Flotsam and Jetsam. After exiting Metallica in 2002, he played with a number of acts, including Voivod and Rock Star Supernova, as well as a touring stint with Ozzy Osbourne, and his current project, the "stoner punk-metal" combo Papa Wheelie, which, at press time, has yet to record.

There are other branches on the Metallica family tree, some that even extend out well past just music.

Climb high.

CORROSION OF CONFORMITY (C.O.C.)

Rowdy knockabouts from Raleigh, North Carolina, Corrosion of Conformity hit the pits as a hardcore ensemble in the early '80s, evolved toward thrash, promoted rhythm guitarist Pepper Keenan to front man (after advertising, unsuccessfully, for a singer who sounded like James Hetfield), and, by decade's end, emerged as an ongoing favorite of Metallica and Metallica fans alike.

Corrosion of Conformity—colloquially, C.O.C.—shed much of their punk sound and bubbled just below the mainstream throughout the early '90s (benefitting, no doubt, from Metallica's Black Album steamrolling existing obstacles).

Deliverance, C.O.C.'s 1994 album, crackles with heavy Southern rock in the mold of classic Molly Hatchet and contemporaries Nashville Pussy (even the title embraces the band's down-home lineage by invoking the hillbilly sodomy movie classic). It was a hit.

They scored even bigger two years later with *Wiseblood*, featuring James Hetfield himself supplying backup vocals on the track "Man or Ash." Pepper returned the favor by playing and taking a verse on the cover of "Tuesday's Gone" by Lynyrd Skynyrd on Metallica's *Garage Inc.* album.

C.O.C. then opened for Metallica on their 1996 tour.

The most dramatic commingling of the groups is on display in the documentary *Some Kind of Monster*, where Pepper competes against Suicidal Tendencies' Robert Trujillo and Marilyn Manson's Jeordie White (aka Twiggy Ramirez) to fill Metallica's bassist slot recently vacated by Jason Newsted.

The gig (and $1 million signing bonus) ultimately went to Trujillo, but C.O.C. soldiers on.

These days, Pepper's not always with C.O.C., as he's focused more on Down, the pitch-black Southern-sludge-metal supergroup featuring Pantera's Phil Anselmo, Jimmy Bower of Eyehategod, and Kirk Windstein and Todd Strange of Crowbar.

Metallica fans should not only check out Down's remarkable canon, but the extreme works of all its individual members.

Remember that Metallica itself came from—and expanded—

metal's outermost reaches. Even now, keeping up with those new frontiers keeps the band on top of their game. Join them in that continuing exploration.

ECHOBRAIN

"Echobrain is the future," Lars Ulrich dismally moans in the documentary *Some Kind of Monster*. It's right after he and record producer Bob Rock have just witnessed thirteen-year Metallica bassist Jason Newsted perform with this new group, the one for which he, in essence, left the biggest hard rock band in the history of the world.

Ulrich and Rock then wait around to congratulate Newsted, but the wayward bass-master has left the building, moving on to the future. Which was not, it turned out, Echobrain.

Initially conceived at Newsted's 1995 Super Bowl party and featuring literal kids-next-door Brian Sagrafena and Dylan Donkin, Echobrain's self-titled 2002 debut boasts cameos by Kirk Hammett and Faith No More's Jim Martin. Don't let that fool you into thinking it's metal, though.

Echobrain by Echobrain instead, is lilting, unhurried, jazzy in some spots, poppy in others, and groovily hippie-ish in spirit. It is also solidly rooted in rock, however, and technically top-notch.

Also, this opening shot would also be Newsted's Echobrain swan song.

Sans the bass behemoth, Echobrain recorded a follow-up album and opened for Neil Young. Then they stopped.

Echobrain did leave behind one record that, while pleasant, would be largely unremarkable if it weren't so hugely remarkable as a glimpse into Jason Newsted's psyche that Metallica fans would likely otherwise never have gotten.

FLOTSAM AND JETSAM

Arizona thrash act Flotsam and Jetsam might be remembered as worthwhile contemporaries of up-and-coming Metallica even if they weren't the band that bassist Jason Newsted left in 1987 to fill the slot tragically opened by the death of Cliff Burton.

But, alas, Flotsam and Jetsam is that band and, as such, it's one of the most crucial roots of the Metallica family tree.

F&J's acclaimed debut, *Doomsday for the Deceiver*, in fact, is the only album on which Newsted plays. He also wrote most of the lyrics. The music is impressively thrashy, alluding subtly to Dark Angel and, both subtly and not, to Metallica. Perhaps most remarkably, Doomsday turns up on-screen in *Sleepaway Camp II: Unhappy Campers* (1988).

The follow-up, *No Place for Disgrace*, garnered its share of MTV *Headbangers Ball* play with its cover of Elton John's "Saturday Night's All Right for Fighting," but by then F&J were destined to remain permanently in Metallica's shadow.

After more albums and another significant departure (Newsted replacement Troy Gregory quit to play with industrial NYC outfit Prong in '92), recognition and success continually proved elusive to Flotsam.

Still, the band kept at it. And it still does today.

PANSY DIVISION

Homo-riffic San Francisco "queercore" outfit Pansy Division can boast a one-of-a-kind guest guitar solo by "Al Shitonia"—aka Kirk Hammett—on their 1997 track titled, fittingly (in every sense), "Headbanger."

Appropriately, this went down (pun, as always intended) during Kirk's mascara phase.

Oh, the man-on-manity!

ROCK STAR SUPERNOVA

The premise of the 2006 CBS game show *Rock Star: Supernova* was the search for an unknown rock star to front a band—consisting of Guns N' Roses' Gilby Clarke, Mötley Crüe's Tommy Lee, and Metallica's Jason Newsted—called Supernova.

A long-running pop-punk trio named Supernova slammed a legal kibosh on that, and thus reality TV's contribution to heavy metal ventured forth, led by contest winner Lukas Rossi, as Rock Star Supernova.

Seeing how so clunky a moniker should not be further complicated, the group's one and only album is self-titled. Not that anybody bought it anyway (or even—be still, Lars—downloaded it on Napster.

Rock Star Supernova is as calculated for radio saturation and chain-store unit-moving as you'd expect, and while that has worked great for boob-tube bubblegum pop (the Monkees, the Archies, the Partridge Family), it is a formula loath to alchemize with heavy metal.

The single "Headspin" sums up the entire album. It's almost a power ballad, shot through with tepid techno, and it gets metallicized by Nine Inch Nails–style sheets of black guitar on the chorus. Somewhere in that mix, Jason Newsted (we're told) is playing bass.

If you like Metallica, it behooves you to investigate the band's least likely offshoot. And Rock Star Supernova it is.

SPASTIK CHILDREN

Metallica's punk side never got punkier than in this loose-limbed, no-rehearsals-allowed slop-core ensemble that occasionally crashed Northern California dives throughout the '80s.

Featuring James Hetfield on drums and, at various times, Cliff Burton, Kirk Hammett, and Jason Newsted on bass, Spastik Children also included Big Jim Martin of Faith No More on lead guitar, Doug Piercy of Heathen on rhythm, and occasional vomit-vocals power-booted by Exodus front-monster Paul Baloff.

The Spastik songbook includes "Let Me Flush," "What's That Smell?" and "Thermos," a cover of the ditty Steve Martin sings while bathing in *The Jerk* (1979).

YouTube is loaded with live clips, most of which are of appropriately crappy quality.

SUICIDAL TENDENCIES

Skateboarding, spray-painting, slashing, and headbanging their way to the big time from the scary streets of Venice, California,

Suicidal Tendencies has always been as much a lifestyle as it is a band. And it's one hell of a band.

Muscle-bound front man Mike Muir initially intended Suicidal Tendencies to be a "party band," but his own performance intensity, coupled with the band's heavier-than-hardcore sound, simply did not allow the music to function solely as a good-time soundtrack.

Adding gravitas was Muir's trademark low-riding blue bandana and the particularly dramatic violence that surrounded the group's performances. In time, Suicidal Tendencies would figure as one of the great conduits of the metal-punk crossover but, at first, the cultures they bridged were those of fistfight-prone early-'80s hardcore kids and Latino gang members from their native Venice.

In fact, an actual criminal street gang cropped up around the band: the Suicidal Cycos (commonly known as "Suicidals" or "Suis"). Few, if any, other rock groups can claim that level of lethal admirer dedication.

What's remarkable is that for all this real-world tumult and destruction, Suicidal Tendencies are often riotously funny.

The band's breakthrough singles "I Saw Your Mommy" and "Institutionalized" address deadly serious topics—parental suicide and teenage mental illness—with cheeky lyrics so overstated as to be subtle. The words are then alternately babbled and roared over jarringly witty tempo changes. To hear the songs' sudden accelerations and drop-offs is to laugh even (especially in the mid-'80s) if you're not sure why.

"I Saw Your Mommy" (the next line is "and your mommy is dead!") was an instant high school sing-along favorite. "Institutionalized" became a heavy-rotation MTV staple in 1984, at a time when no other hardcore got played in the channel's prime time. It also figures prominently in the cult film *Repo Man* (1984) and even on an episode of NBC's *Miami Vice*.

While Metallica remained quarantined in the headbanger ghetto, Suicidal Tendencies was sneaking punk and metal sounds and attitudes into the mainstream. In turn, there's no denying that these wild Venice locos absorbed much of what Metallica was up to at the same time.

The 1987 Suicidal Tendencies album *Join the Army* angered many fans upon first listen, as it was "too metal." Some fled, but many more got pulled into the Suicidal loop.

By the time Muir hired Anthrax producer Mark Dodson to oversee his group's major label debut, *How Can I Laugh Tomorrow When I Can't Even Smile Today*, Suicidal Tendencies may have had one boot planted more firmly in the metal camp than in their punk past, but they used both to stomp forward.

Like that of many bands, Suicidal's lineup remained ever rotating. Muir was the one constant. He added the perfect piece to complete the ultimate Suicidal Tendencies configuration in 1989: a bassist billed at first as Stymee, who later went by his given name, Robert Trujillo.

The Mexican-American Trujillo infused Suicidal with funk stylings and musical complexity that pushed outward toward prog rock. His Hulk-in-a-bounce-house stage presence provided a perfect foil for that of the peripatetic Muir.

The newly inspired group's acclaimed, best-selling 1990 album *Lights . . . Camera . . . Revolution* hit at the perfect moment, just as rock's fringes kicked down the mainstream's gates to become the mainstream itself. It stands as one of the key records that readied MTV and FM radio for the likes of Metallica's Black Album a year hence.

Muir and Trujillo even embarked on popular side project together, the funk metal outfit Infectious Grooves.

Throughout 1993 and '94, Suicidal Tendencies opened for on Metallica on tour. They were not just veterans now; they were dangerously close to becoming rock royalty.

Taking the exact opposite approach of Metallica, Muir shunned such top-tier success by issuing the berserk, obscene *Suicidal for Life* album. It not only sold poorly and alienated fans, it tore the group apart.

Shortly thereafter, Robert Trujillo found new employment in Ozzy Osbourne's band.

Eight years later, he got another gig. In Metallica.

Suicidal Tendencies, meanwhile, regrouped in 1997, released a few more albums and, with an occasional break, have been touring ever since.

They're keeping it real. With or without Robert Trujillo.

VOIVOD

Launched from some unknown orb spinning in some uncharted nook of the universe, Voivod first touched down on our planet by way of Quebec, Canada, circa 1982.

Like Metallica, Voivod took supreme inspiration from old-school hard rock, the New Wave of British Heavy Metal, and punk. As a result, their first few records thrash admirably. But this Canuck foursome's hearts burned hottest for prog giants on the order of Pink Floyd, King Crimson, and Rush.

In 1987, Voivod got to join that pantheon upon their release of *Killing Technology*, the first installment in a virtuoso musical sci-fi cycle that continued over the next two years with *Dimension Hatross* and *Nothingface*, the last of which garnered high public praise from Metallica bassist Jason Newsted.

The 1990s proved problematic for Voivod, with key members coming and going, and replacement vocalist and bassist Eric Forrest becoming incapacitated due to a car accident over which the group was sued by his insurance company.

After performing and recording with varying degrees of success, three of Voivod's four founders returned to the group in 2002: singer Denis Belanger (aka Snake), guitarist Denis D'Amour (aka Piggy), and drummer Michel Lanevin (aka Away). Joining them on bass was newly de-Metallica'd Jason Newsted (aka Jasonic, aka Jason Newkid—yet again).

This Voivod incarnation played together for three years, stopped only by Piggy's tragic 2005 demise from colon cancer. *Katorz*, released the next year, was based on notes and riffs Piggy left behind, as well as instructions he gave the group from his deathbed.

With Piggy gone, Jason Newsted took leave of Voivod, too, but the band plays on, a testament to what talent, vision, perseverance—and having a huge fan in Metallica—can accomplish.

THE CALL OF KTULU
H. P. Lovecraft

Howard Phillips Lovecraft (1890–1937) ranks among the most influential, consequential, and personally mysterious authors in all of literature. In the realms of horror, science fiction, and fantasy, he is revered as a god—albeit a dark, damned, and damning one, befitting the universe and mythology Lovecraft concocted through his writing.

Metallica's "Call of Ktulu" is an instrumental tribute to Lovecraft's iconic story "The Call of Cthulu." While some say that the band simply misspelled the name of the cosmically evil title creature, who is described as resembling "an octopus, a dragon, and a human caricature [with] . . . rudimentary wings."

The story makes clear, though, that saying Cthulu's name out loud brings him closer to you, and hence Metallica intentionally screwed up the letters as "Ktulu." That's also why the song has no lyrics.

"The Thing That Should Not Be" is Metallica's other Lovecraft homage, inspired by the story "The Shadow over Innsmouth." The title refers to Dagon, a sinister undersea deity and compatriot of Cthulu who terrorizes a seaside town.

The scary, funny, and exciting fright film *Dagon* (2001) is based on the same work, and it also functions as a cinematically fleshed-out version of "The Thing That Should Not Be."

Dagon was directed by Stuart Gordon, the great interpreter of H. P. Lovecraft for the screen. No Metallica fan should be unacquainted with Gordon's masterpiece, the splatter classic *Re-Animator* (1985), nor its underrated follow-up *From Beyond* (1986), both of which are based on Lovecraft pieces.

More importantly, discover or return to Lovecraft's written works. Dive deep into what inspired not only Metallica and Stuart Gordon, but Stephen King—who credits Lovecraft with initially sparking his interest in horror—and no less than Black Sabbath, whose "Behind the Wall of Sleep" is homage to Lovecraft's "Beyond the Wall of Sleep."

Other rock tributes to H. P. Lovecraft have come from Dream Theater,

Morbid Angel, the Black Dahlia Murder, the Fall, and a metal-friendly psychedelic prog act from the '60s and '70s that called itself, simply, H. P. Lovecraft.

Call it Cthulu at your own risk (or play it safe like Metallica and say "Ktulu"), but the vast, foreboding world of H. P. Lovecraft is an extension of the heavy metal universe you must investigate.

LULU
Marianne Faithfull

At first, Marianne Faithfull contributing to Metallica's "The Memory Remains" seemed nearly as inexplicable as the band later announcing they were making an album with Lou Reed.

Well, okay, it wasn't that baffling but, still, the only female vocals to ever be included on a Metallica song are simply a repeated half-chant of variations on "die-da-da-die-die-da."

Why?

More specifically, why did it have to be done in the tobacco-hammered mummy croak of Marianne Faithfull?

Lars told MTV: "It started dawning on us that maybe having a character on the song would be a good thing, somebody playing the part created for the scenario of the song. We said we need someone charismatic, someone who is weathered in every way. So I called up [Marianne] and said it would mean a lot to us if she would sing on the record and she did."

Charismatic and weathered, Marianne Faithfull most definitely can do.

She initially caught on as a folkie songbird who scored a hit in 1964 by covering the Stones' "As Tears Go By." And then the Rolling Stones covered her—literally.

"My first move was to get a Rolling Stone as a boyfriend," Faithfull told *New Musical Express* in 1966. "I slept with three and decided the lead singer was the best bet."

Mick Jagger credits Faithfull as the inspiration for "You Can't Always Get What You Want" and "Wild Horses." Her role as muse further extended to the Beatles, who wrote "And Your Bird Can Sing" about her, and Graham Nash, whose "Carrie Ann" (instead of "Marianne," get it?) was a hit for his group the Hollies.

There's a ton of rock history in Marianne Faithfull's throat.

EYE OF THE BEHOLDER
Visual Artists Pushead and Andres Serrano

Visual artists and hard rock share a storied, mutually beneficial history.

Where might Iron Maiden be, for example, without illustrator Derek Riggs's punk zombie portrait turned all-time reigning metal superhero Eddie the Head?

Pulp genius Frank Frazetta painted unforgettable album covers for Molly Hatchet, Nazareth, Dust, and Yngwie Malmstein.

The Ramones were often defined by the doodles by multitalented *Punk* magazine publisher John Holmstrom adorning their T-shirts and liner notes.

Black Flag's musical impact was aided immeasurably by artist Raymond Pettibon's iconic four-bar logo and stark, madness-inflamed drawings on all the band's records.

Metallica's logo was actually designed by James Hetfield, but for the bulk of their eye-popping imagery, they turned to the talent who had bestowed the "Crimson Ghost" mascot upon the Misfits: skate-rat wonderworker Brian Schroeder, better known by the tag Pushead.

In 1986, Hetfield went skating with Pushead and the singer broke his arm, costing Metallica what would have been an almost unimaginable opportunity to perform "Master of Puppets" on *Saturday Night Live*.

Proving that there were clearly no hard feelings, Metallica put Pushead to work for them as he rendered many of their most memorable images, including the jackets of the albums . . . *And Justice for All* and

St. Anger, plus the singles "One," "Harvester of Sorrow," and "Eye of the Beholder," and the video covers for *Cliff 'Em All* and *A Year and a Half in the Life of Metallica*.

Aside from fronting hardcore reprobates Septic Death and putting out records by punk-metal self-destructors Poison Idea, Pushead provided artwork for Metallica compatriots that include Corrosion of Conformity, S.O.D., Queensrÿche, Prong, Kylesa, Necros, Chaos UK, and, as mentioned, the many undertakings of Glenn Danzig.

Among the many controversies surrounding Metallica's *Load* and *ReLoad* releases was the records' departure from the sort of artwork (usually by Pushead) that fans had come to expect.

The band opted, instead, to go highbrow. Okay, Lars and Kirk opted for fruit-bat New York snob nonsense, while James and Jason kept their traps shut.

Both *Load* and *ReLoad* boast covers by snooty, big-money culture "bad boy" Andres Serrano. Prior to Metallica, Serrano had been best known for dropping a crucifix in a cup of yellowish fluid, taking a picture of it, and calling it "Piss Christ."

Turtlenecked sub-C.H.U.D.s in Manhattan galleries couldn't crack open their wallets quick enough.

Fortunately or unfortunately (and you know which way most Metallica fans veer), Kirk was among those impressed. The cover of *Load* is an abstract Serrano photograph titled *Blood and Semen III* that Kirk saw in a book he bought at a museum. It's a blob of red and black nothing that, the foo-foo racketeer claims, was created by pressing cow blood and his own jizz between two sheets of Plexiglas.

Sure.

ReLoad is wrapped in an even less engaging Serrano snapshot that's just called *Blood and Piss*.

Sure and sure again.

THIS WAS JUST YOUR LIFE
Fourteen Metallica Tribute Albums

Throughout its life span, Metallica has covered songs that the band loves by artists they respect. On these following records, devotees paid Metallica a huge compliment in return.

Apocalyptica Plays Metallica by Four Cellos (1997)—Apocalyptica
Finnish Metallica fanatics who happen to be master cellists, Apocalyptica deliver mammoth bow-swept power in each of these eight covers.

Bite the Ivory: Piano Tribute to Metallica (2008)—Vitamin Piano Series
Metal's heaviest four-piece gets run through the old eighty-eight keys.

The Celtic Tribute to Metallica (2008)—Various Artists
Delving as deep as the roots of Metallica's version of "Whiskey in the Jar" can go, this Celtic tribute reworks a roster of neck-snapper by way of accordion, banjo, fiddle, pennywhistle, mandolin, and concertina. Oh, and also: lots and lots of beer.

Fade to Bluegrass: Bluegrass Tribute to Metallica (2003)—Iron Horse
Plunk, plunk, plunk go the power chords, leading to plink-plink-plink leads and solos on *Fade to Bluegrass*'s banjos and mandolins. The pining, lonely harmonies lend themselves to the original lyrics surprisingly well. A *Volume 2* followed in 2006.

Harptallica: A Tribute (2007)—Harptallica
Two female harp players bang their fingers, recreating Metallica songs on the lightest-sounding, but heaviest-weighing of all actually metal instruments.

Hip-Hop Tribute to Metallica (2005)—Various Artists
Masterminded by producer Brian Bart, this hip-hop tribute show-cases rappers Cee and Rhashidi, as they rhythmically belt out words by James Hetfield and grooves by everybody else in the band.

Metallica Assault (2001)—Various Artists
Metal superstars convene in ten different pickup configurations to take on Metallica classics. Among the dream-team players are Dave

Lombardo and a young Robert Trujillo on "Battery"; Scott Ian, Vinny Appice, and Billy Milano on "Whiplash"; Burton C. Bell and John Christ on "Enter Sandman"; Lemmy playing bass on "Nothing Else Matters"; and Blue Öyster Cult's Eric Bloom singing lead on "For Whom the Bell Tolls."

Metallic Attack: Metallica—The Ultimate Tribute (2005)—Various Artists

Another all-star metal roster roaring through ten Metallica biggies. Not to be missed is Motörhead's Grammy-winning cover of "Whiplash," Flotsam and Jetsam's "Damage Inc.," Death Angel's "Trapped Under Ice," or Dark Angel's "Creeping Death." Musicians on the other tracks include Scott Ian, Nuno Bettencourt, Joe Lynn Turner, Eric Singer, and Page Hamilton of Helmet.

Pianotarium: Piano Tribute to Metallica (2007)—Scott D. Davis

Another set of ivories takes another Metallica-powered pounding.

Punk Tribute to Metallica (2001)—Various Artists

A project that seemed like a natural, punks being punky and all, it took a long time to reach fruition. Fortunately, it's worth it. Highlights: "Jump in the Fire" by Dee Dee Ramone, "Seek and Destroy" by Agent Orange, "Sad but True" by Flipper, "Motorbreath" by D.O.A., and "Nothing Else Matters" by the Vibrators.

Say Your Prayers, Little One: String Quartet Tribute to Metallica (2003)—The Angry String Orchestra

Same basic idea as Apocalyptica, but relatively lackluster in execution. For completists.

The Scorched Earth Orchestra Plays Metallica's Master of Puppets (2006)—Scorched Earth Orchestra

Lush, booming, and taking the orchestral majesty inherent within *Master of Puppets* to its literal incarnation, The Scorched Earth Orchestra have created, by way of an entire album cover, something massively original.

Sgt. Hetfield's Motorbreath Pub Ban (2007)—Beatallica

Headbanging mop-top spoofsters from Milwaukee mash up Metallica with the Beatles. The two follow-up albums are *All You Need Is Blood* (2008) and *Masterful Mystery Tour* (2009).

Tribute to Metallica (1993)—Die Krupps

German industrial giants Die Krupps up the metal, in a literal sense, among Metallica's heavy in the first of series of thumping, pumping covers collections.

THE OFFICIAL
HEAVY METAL
BOOK OF LISTS

ERIC DANVILLE

ILLUSTRATIONS BY CLIFF MOTT
FOREWORD BY LEMMY

10

READ THE LIGHTNING:
THE BEST BOOKS TO CRACK OPEN…
IF YOU LIKE METALLICA

Reading is fun for mentals. These books made that plain. Powerfully so.

BIOGRAPHIES, MEMOIRS, AND HISTORY BOOKS

The Encyclopaedia Metallica
By Malcolm Dome and Jerry Ewing
(CHROME DREAMS, 2007)
A fine, quick primer on the Metalliverse, most useful as a catalyst for more in-depth research.

Enter Night: A Biography of Metallica
By Mick Wall
(ST. MARTIN'S, 2010)
Battle-hardened rock journalist Mick Wall gives Metallica the expansive, opinionated overview that he'd done previously in tomes on Iron Maiden, Pearl Jam, Bono (yecch), disc jockey John Peel, and multiple volumes on Black Sabbath and Guns N' Roses. It's a terrific read.

Justice for All: The Truth About Metallica
By Joel McIver
(OMNIBUS PRESS, 2009)
Exhaustive, obsessive, and epic. The bible of Metallibios.

Metallica: All That Matters
By Paul Stenning
(PLEXUS PUBLISHING, 2009)
Fact by fact, quote by quote, *All That Matters* is a serviceable (enough) bio from a writer who's produced similar media-store shelf-units on AC/DC, Slash, My Chemical Romance, Rage Against the Machine and, yes, *Twilight* dreamboat Robert Pattinson.

Metallica: The Frayed Ends of Metal
By Chris Crocker
(ST. MARTIN'S GRIFFIN, 1992)
Interesting as a snapshot of Metallica post–Black Album, pre-haircuts, and at the top of a very rapidly (and permanently) changing game.

Metallica: The Stories Behind the Biggest Songs
By Chris Ingham
(CARLTON BOOKS, 2009)
Nicely selected compendium of anecdotes.

Metallica: This Monster Lives—The Inside Story of Some Kind of Monster
By Joel Berlinger with Greg Milner
(ST. MARTIN'S GRIFFIN, 2004)
Up close and inside the making, and aftermath, of the landmark documentary.

Metallica Unbound
By K. J. Doughton
(GRAND CENTRAL PUBLISHING, 1993)
That's a kick-ass title, to which the text and generous allotment of photographs ably live up. Stopping after the Black Album's mushroom cloud and metallic fallout, *Unbound* is a weighty book, suitable for stopping doors, slamming skulls, and even just reading.

Mustaine: A Heavy Metal Memoir
By Dave Mustaine
(Harper Collins, 2010)
Eminently readable and clearly in its author's voice, *Mustaine* is indispensible to fans of Metallica, Megadeth, and the man himself. Interestingly, I liked Dave less as an overall human being after reading his memoir, but that only made me appreciate his candor all the more.

To Live Is to Die: The Life and Death of Metallica's Cliff Burton
By Joel McIver
(Jawbone Press, 2009)
Joel McIver, author of the relentlessly researched and expertly executed *Justice for All*, focuses strictly on Metallica's fallen angel. The result is heartwarming, heartbreaking, and headbanging all at once.

THEORY AND PHILOSOPHY

Damage Incorporated: Metallica and the Production of Musical Identity
By Glenn T. Pillsbury
(Routledge, 2006)
Weighty and academic. If you're writing a term paper, here lies plenty to crib.

The Day Metallica Came to Church
By John Van Sloten
(Faith Alive Christian Resources, 2010)
You read that publisher's name right. Pastor John Van Sloten links the lyrics and vibe of his (and our) favorite metal band to the teachings of the New Testament. You may come away believing that the *H* in Jesus H. Christ stands for "heavy."

Heavy Metal: The Music and Its Culture

By Deena Weinstein

(DA CAPO, 2000)

Sociologist Deena Weinstein casts her Ivy League gaze upon the leather-and-head-injury set. The first edition was published in 1991, to some degree of fanfare in decidedly non-metal circles. As is typical of this form of outsider-attempting-to-be-an-expert writing, Weinstein begins with an agenda and assembles the facts to make her case. She's pro-headbanger, and headbangers, in turn, are likely to emerge pro-Deena.

Metallica and Philosophy: A Crash Course in Brain Surgery

Edited by William Irwin

(BLACKWELL PUBLISHING, 2010)

Heady concepts translated for lay thinkers (in every respect). Multiple professors and essayists cast Metallica in light of history's most cerebral heavyweights, and the end product is thought-provoking and, often, downright fun—even for a three-time college dropout like me. Editor William Irwin has assembled other titles in this series on The Simpsons, Seinfeld, Watchmen, True Blood, The Matrix, and more. That he selected Metallica as the sole rock group in the canon displays his good taste. You can let him out of his locker now.

Rock and the Pop Narcotic: Testament for the Electric Church

By Joe Carducci

(2.13.61, 1995)

Originally going off like a concussion bomb in 1991 (year of the Black Album), rescued in an updated volume by Henry Rollins's now defunct press, and most recently reissued by some fly-by-night operation in 2005, *Rock and the Pop*

Narcotic is the sound of a mad genius napalming the path to a new god by way of goddamned rock 'n' roll. Joe Carducci worked at SST Records in the '80s, and his thesis is that the two greatest rock bands of all time are Black Sabbath and Black Flag, and the reason they're not universally recognized as such is due to an East Coast rock critic conspiracy that forces Springsteen and U2 on us, the lowly benighted, in hopes that some day we will at least try to be as decent and lofty a breed of heroes as East Coast rock critics fancy themselves to be. There is more—so much more—to *RATPN* than that, including an artist-by-artist history of the medium's most visionary prophets (Metallica among them) and a political point of view that is absolutely taboo in the realm of rockcritocracy. Carducci fires his zealotry with such impact and style that delving into this Talmud is like getting shot in the face point-blank with a bazooka. He is also amazingly hilarious.

This Ain't the Summer of Love: Conflict and Crossover in Heavy Metal and Punk
By *Steve Waksman*
(UNIVERSITY OF CALIFORNIA PRESS, 2009)
Steve Waksman begins rock history here with the Stooges and Sabbath and moves forward under the notion that what resulted were not separate camps of "punk" and "metal" (or as it is most often cast, "punk" versus "metal"), but one continuum of heavy music in which those camps are inseparably intertwined. A solid idea, well played.

PHOTO BOOKS

Metallica, Club Dayz 1982–1984
By *Bill Hale*
(ECW PRESS, 2009)
Vintage looks at the boys when they were still just, indeed, boys.

Murder in the Front Row: Shots from the Bay Area Thrash Metal Epicenter

By Harold Oimoen and Brian Lew

(Bazillion Points, 2011)

The masters at Bazillion Points have assembled a brilliant, breathtaking coffee-table book here, with great writing and photography so sharp, you may come away bloodied—but satisfied.

So What: The Good, the Mad, and the Ugly

By Metallica and Steffan Chirazi

(Broadway Books)

So what? It's Metallica's authorized photo history, that's what. It's huge, beautiful, and essential.

The Ultimate Metallica

By Ross Halfin

(Chronicle Books, 2010)

Legendary shutterbug Ross Halfin began shooting Metallica from their earliest shows onward. This glossy volume assembles a quarter-century of his masterful snapshots.

HARD ROCK AND HEAVY METAL

Choosing Death: The Improbable History of Death Metal and Grindcore

By Albert Mudrian

(Feral House, 2004)

Bolstered by a forward from metal-boosting DJ John Peel, *Choosing Death* expertly chronicles the six-foot-under term taking by thrash into the extreme-beyond-extreme realm of death metal and the extremer-than-beyond-extreme grindcore.

Eddie Trunk's Essential Hard Rock and Heavy Metal

By Eddie Trunk

(Abrams Image, 2011)

Beloved syndicated metal DJ and TV host of *That Metal Show* Eddie Trunk compiles his personal pics, reminiscences, and outspoken analysis from his up-close-and-personal flesh-pressing with hard rock royalty over multiple decades.

The Encyclopedia of Heavy Metal
By Daniel Bukszpan
(STERLING, 2003)
Somebody had to write it, and Daniel Bukszpan pulls it off pretty okay.

Heavy Metal Movies: The 666 Most Headbanging Films of All Time
By Mike McPadden
(BAZILLION POINTS, 2012)
From Anvil to Zardoz, Brooklyn-born Chicago-noise bozo Mike McPadden lays bare the naked truth of the metal-blackened silver screen. If you've made it this far, you may already be a fan of the author.

Lords of Chaos: The Bloody Rise of the Satanic Metal Underground
By Michael Moynihan and Didrik Soderlind
(FERAL HOUSE, 2003)
Corpse paint and church arson! Suicide and cannibalism! Murder and mayhem and the band Mayhem! *Lords of Chaos* is often criticized by those with a stake (pun intended) in the black metal game, but none of them answered with a more definitive summation of this most insular of extreme scene's Norway-led legions of indecency. It's to be a major motion picture but, since that announcement was made years ago, probably not soon.

Mean Deviation: Four Decades of Progressive Heavy Metal
By Jeff Wagner
(BAZILLION POINTS, 2011)
As a man emblazoned with tattoo tributes to King Crimson,

Butthole Surfers, the Melvins, and Meat Loaf, I had high hopes for any book documenting metal's most adventurous and exploratory offshoots. Jeff Wagner, former editor of *Metal Maniacs* magazine, makes a perfect starship captain for this psychonaut expedition that includes stops on the planets Rush, Voivod, Celtic Frost, and numerous other prog-metal monoliths who proved crucial to Metallica.

Metalion: The Slayer Mag Diaries
By Jon Kristiansen and Tara G. Warrior
(BAZILLION POINTS, 2011)
Beginning in 1985, burly Norwegian Jon Kristiansen chronicled the black metal revolution from flaming-church ground zero in his typewritten, photocopied zine named, in part, after one of his favorite rising American bands, *Slayer*. Kristiansen wrote under the pen name "Metalion," and he was there for black metal's most notorious arsons, suicide, murder, and cannibalism—in fact, those involved were among his closest friends. Slayer covered the rest of the metal world, too, including the rise and rise of Metallica. Bazillion Points' mammoth hardcover tome *Metalion: The Slayer Mag Diaries* contains every issue of the zine's legendary run, interspersed with chapters of Kristiansen's moving, unflinching memoir that details his coming-of-age when metal's most maniacal happenings were all going down. In every sense, this book is a work of art.

The Official Heavy Metal Book of Lists
By Eric Danville
(BACKBEAT BOOKS, 2009)
Eric Danville, who is also the author of the brilliant porn star biography *The Complete Linda Lovelace*, trades oral sex for aural sets in an eclectic amalgam of rundowns from myriad metal fans on a multitude of heavy topics. Big fun.

Sound of the Beast: The Complete Headbanging History of Heavy Metal
By Ian Christe
(HARPER COLLINS, 2003)

If you are new to heavy metal, get this book. If you are familiar with heavy metal, get this book. If you are an expert on heavy metal, get this book. If you like Metallica, get this book. If you are a member of Metallica, get this book. Get the point? Get this book.

Stairway to Hell: The 500 Greatest Heavy Metal Albums in the Universe
By Chuck Eddy
(DA CAPO, 1998) ORIGINALLY PUBLISHED IN 1991

On one cloven hoof, I am loath to recommend anything claiming to compile the "greatest heavy metal" anything wherein the author brags about how it contains no Iron Maiden or Judas Priest albums. On the other hand, Chuck Eddy's amphetamines-on-speed (get it?) writing style shook me to my every fiber when I first discovered him in 1986 via an article in the *Village Voice* where he declared both Rush and Hüsker Dü to be "the greatest band in the world." *Stairway to Hell* is Eddy's magnum opus, and it is insulting, dismissing, unqualified, off-base, and an outright affront to fans of actual heavy metal. But, for twenty years now, this book has never left the top of my toilet tank, so I always have it close by for inspiration (exactly when I need it most). So consider that Chuck Eddy ranks a record by Teena Marie (yes, the '80s "Lovergirl" one-hitter) in the Top Ten and that he proclaims Kix "the greatest guitar band of the '80s" and then consider how perfect that is from a guy who gushed pure pride over a piece of hate mail that declared: "Chuck Eddy is the mayor of Asshole City."

Swedish Death Metal
By Daniel Ekeroth
(BAZILLION POINTS, 2008)
Obsessive native Daniel Ekeroth documents his homeland's explosion of extreme metal with wit, flair, and you-are-there intensity.

ST. ANGER
The Complete Works of Martin Popoff

Insanely prolific Canuck noggin-knocker Martin Popoff is the cofounder of the crucial metal journal *Brave Words and Bloody Knuckles*, and the author of an astonishing array of bios, review guides, and other indispensible hard rock compendia.

For Metallica fans, Popoff's byline means an automatically worthy read.

Here are this Toronto scribe's most Metalli-pertinent published works.

Black Sabbath: Doom Let Loose
ECW Press, 2006

Black Sabbath FAQ: All That's Left to Know on the First Name in Metal
Backbeat Books, 2011

The Collector's Guide to Heavy Metal Volume 1: The Seventies
Collector's Guide Publishing, 2003

The Collector's Guide to Heavy Metal Volume 2: The Eighties
Collector's Guide Publishing, 2005

The Collector's Guide to Heavy Metal Volume 3: The Nineties
Collector's Guide Publishing, 2007

The Collector's Guide to Heavy Metal Volume 4: The '00s
Collector's Guide Publishing, 2011

Contents Under Pressure: 30 Years of Rush at Home and Away
ECW Press, 2004

Dio: Light Beyond the Black
Metal Blade, 2006

Getting Tighter: Deep Purple '68–'76
Power Chord Press, 2008

Heavy Metal: 20th Century Rock and Roll
Collector's Guide Publishing, 2000

Judas Priest: Heavy Metal Painkillers
ECW Press, 2007

Riff Kills Man!: 25 Years of Recorded Hard Rock and Heavy Metal
Power Chord Press, 1993

Run for Cover: The Art of Derek Riggs
Aardvark Publishing, 2006

Southern Rock Review
Collector's Guide Publishing, 2001

The Top 500 Heavy Metal Albums of All Time
ECW Press, 2004

UFO: Shoot Out the Lights
Metal Blade, 2005

INDEX

If You Like Series

The If You Like series plays the game of cultural connectivity at a high level—each book is written by an expert in the field and travels far beyond the expected, unearthing treats that will enlighten even the most jaded couch potato or pop culture vulture.

If You Like the Beatles...
Here Are Over 200 Bands, Films, Records, and Other Oddities That You Will Love
by Bruce Pollock
Backbeat Books
978-1-61713-018-2 • $14.99

If You Like Metallica...
Here Are Over 200 Bands, CDs, Movies, and Other Oddities That You Will Love
by Mike McPadden
Backbeat Books
978-1-61713-038-0 • $14.99

If You Like Monty Python...
Here Are Over 200 Movies, TV Shows and Other Oddities That You Will Love
by Zack Handlen
Limelight Editions
978-0-87910-393-4 • $14.99

If You Like The Terminator...
Here Are Over 200 Movies, TV Shows, and Other Oddities That You Will Love
by Scott Von Doviak
Limelight Editions
978-0-87910-397-2 • $14.99

If You Like The Sopranos...
Here Are Over 150 Movies, TV Shows, and Other Oddities That You Will Love
by Leonard Pierce
Limelight Editions
978-0-87910-390-3 • $14.99